CRIMINOLOGY

An Introduction Using MicroCase®

Third Edition

by

Rodney Stark
University of Washington

Software Created by
MicroCase Corporation

MicroCase Corporation
Bellevue, Washington

CRIMINOLOGY: An Introduction Using MicroCase, 3rd edition, is published by MicroCase Corporation.

Editor	David Smetters
Text Design and Layout	Jodi B. Gleason
Copy Editor	Margaret Moore
Editorial Assistant	R. K. Clancy
Map and Graphics Editor	June B. Tandy

© 1995 by MicroCase Corporation, All rights reserved.

No part of this book may be reproduced, stored in a retrieval system, or transcribed, in any form or by any means, electronic, mechanical, photocopying, recording, or otherwise, without the prior written permission of the publisher, MicroCase Corporation, 1301 120th Avenue N.E., Bellevue, WA 98005, (206) 635-0293.

IBM PC and IBM-PC DOS are registered trademarks of International Business Machines, Inc. **ShowCase** and **MicroCase** are registered trademarks of MicroCase Corporation.

Printed in the United States of America
1 2 3 4 5 6 7 8 9 10--97 96 95

TABLE OF CONTENTS

About the Author   v
Disclaimer of Warranty   vi

INTRODUCTION

Getting Started   1

PART I: *MEASURING CRIME*

EXERCISE 1	The Geography of Official Crime Rates	3
EXERCISE 2	Victimization and Public Opinion	19
EXERCISE 3	Self-Report Data: Student Samples	31

PART II: *ANALYZING CRIME DATA*

EXERCISE 4	Fear of Violence: Cross-Tabulation	39
EXERCISE 5	Auto Theft: Scatterplots and Correlation	51

PART III: *DRUGS AND ALCOHOL*

EXERCISE 6	Getting Drunk in America	65
EXERCISE 7	Cocaine and Alcohol Abuse: State Rates	81
EXERCISE 8	Alcohol and Drugs in High School	93
EXERCISE 9	Drinking and Doing Drugs in College	103

PART IV: *PROPERTY CRIME*

EXERCISE 10	Burglary Victims	113
EXERCISE 11	Social Disorganization and Property Crime	121
EXERCISE 12	High School Offenders	131
EXERCISE 13	College Offenders	141

PART V: *VIOLENT CRIME*

EXERCISE 14	Analyzing Violent Crime Rates	149
EXERCISE 15	Whose Friends Are Getting Murdered?	159

PART VI: *MULTI-VARIATE ANALYSIS*

EXERCISE 16	Violence and the Old West: Regression	167
EXERCISE 17	"Mass Media" Criminology: Detecting Spuriousness	181

APPENDIX A: *INDEPENDENT PROJECTS*

♦ Gun Control ♦ Capital Punishment   193

APPENDIX B: *CODEBOOKS*

Short Label: NORC	194
Short Label: FIFTYC	194
Short Label: COLLEGEC	195
Short Label: HISCHOOL	195
Long Label: NORC	196
Long Label: FIFTYC	198
Long Label: COLLEGEC	205
Long Label: HISCHOOL	207

Sources

ABOUT THE AUTHOR

Rodney Stark received his Ph.D. from the University of California, Berkeley, where he held full-time research positions in the Survey Research Center and the Center for the Study of Law and Society. At present he is professor of sociology at the University of Washington. He is the author of 14 books and scores of journal articles. In 1993 he received the award for distinguished scholarship from the Pacific Sociological Association.

Disclaimer of Warranty: the licensor warrants that software is provided "as is" and without warranties as to performance or merchantability. Agents of the supplier may have made statements about this software. Any such statements do not constitute warranties and shall not be relied on by the licensee in deciding whether to use this program.

This program is provided without any express or implied warranties whatsoever. Because of the diversity of conditions and hardware under which this program may be used, no warranty of fitness for a particular purpose is offered. The licensee is advised to test the program thoroughly before relying on it. The licensee must assume the entire risk of using the program. Any liability of provider or manufacturer will be limited exclusively to product replacement.

The licensor shall not be liable for any expense, claim, liability, loss, or damage (including any incidental or consequential damage) either direct or indirect, by licensee from the use of the software.

Replacement Disk Policy: *MicroCase*® Corporation will replace any magnetic diskette that proves defective in materials or workmanship. To obtain a replacement copy, please ask your instructor or write to *MicroCase*® Corporation, 1301 120th Avenue N.E., Bellevue, WA 98005. You will be required to return the defective diskette in exchange for a replacement. Should you need to exchange the 5 1/4" diskettes for one that is 3 1/2" (or vice versa) send us your original diskette and $5. (Sorry, we cannot accept credit cards.)

INTRODUCTION

Welcome to the real world of criminological research. There is nothing make-believe about what you will be doing with this student version of MicroCase. All of the data are real. In fact, they are some of the best data available to professional researchers, and you will be using some of the same research techniques they use. As you work through these exercises you will discover a lot of criminology for yourself.

The software is so easy to use that you will learn it without study — just start with the first exercise and follow along. But, despite being easy, this software is not a toy. Its computational heart is the same as that included in the full MicroCase Analysis System.

GETTING STARTED

This student version of MicroCase requires an IBM-PC or fully compatible computer with a graphics card (preferably in color) and 640K of memory.

To begin, make sure your computer is at the DOS system prompt (which looks something like C:>). Then place the diskette in the A or B drive. If you placed the diskette in the A drive, *type A:* and *press <ENTER>*; if you placed the disk in the B drive, *type B:* and *press <ENTER>*. Then *type MC* and *press <ENTER>*. (To use Student MicroCase on a computer with a monochrome display, you may need to start the program by *typing MC MONO* instead of MC.) It will take about 20 seconds to 30 seconds for the program to load.

Important: The first time you start Student MicroCase, you will be asked to enter your name. It is important to type your name correctly, since it will appear on all printed output. Type your name and *press <ENTER>*. If it is correct, simply *press <ENTER>* in response to the next prompt. (If you wish to correct a mistake, *type Y* at the prompt and *press <ENTER>*.) The copyright screen will appear. *Press <ENTER>* to continue.

MicroCase works from two primary menus. If you are using a color monitor, one menu is blue, the other is red. When you enter the program and pass beyond the title screen the blue menu will be on the screen. It looks like this:

```
%%%%%%%%%%%%%%%%%%%%%%% DATA AND FILE MANAGEMENT %%%%%%%%%%%%%%%%%%%%%%%%

*S. Switch To STATISTICAL ANALYSIS MENU

DATA MANAGEMENT:
   A. Define Variables/Recodes           E. Codebook
   B. Collapse/Strip Categories          F. Edit Variable Information
   C. Enter Data from Keyboard           G. Grading Recode
   D. List or Print Variable Values      H. Setup Data Entry

FILE MANAGEMENT:
  *I. Open, Look, Erase or Copy File     M. Move Data between Files
   J. Create New Data File               N. Merge Files
   K. Create Subset File                 O. Create Aggregation File
   L. Import/Export Data                 P. Create Statistical Summary

*X. EXIT from MicroCase
```

Notice that the highlight is on **I. Open, Look, Erase or Copy File**. This is the only task listed on this menu that is available in this version of the program, and that is why there is an asterisk to the left of the letter I. In order to analyze data, you must open a data file. So, *press the <ENTER>* key. The screen now displays the four data files available to you: **COLLEGEC, FIFTYC, HISCHOOL,** and **NORC**. To open a file, place the highlight over its name and *press <ENTER>*. You can always move the highlight around by using the arrow keys. Move the highlight to **FIFTYC**. *Press <ENTER>* to open this file; *press <ENTER>* again to return to the menu.

Notice that the highlight is at the top of the screen on **Switch To STATISTICAL ANALYSIS MENU**. To switch to the second menu, just *press <ENTER>*. You can always move from one menu to the other by typing S. Now you are on the red menu, which looks like this:

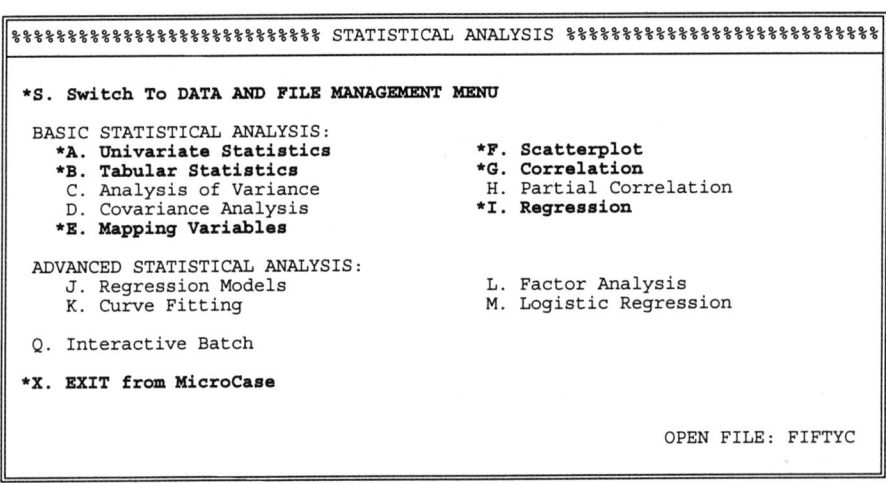

Of these statistical functions, only six are available in this version of the software. Not all six are available at any one time, since several are suitable only for certain kinds of data. For example, mapping and scatterplot functions are useful only with aggregate data such as states, while cross-tabulation is appropriate only for survey data. Thus, what is available on the red screen will depend upon which data set you have open. You can tell which functions are available by noting the asterisks to the left of the names. In the exercises that follow, you will be introduced to each of these functions and learn how to use and interpret each.

When you are finished using MicroCase simply *type X* from the main menu, or put the highlight on **EXIT from MicroCase** and *press <ENTER>*. The exit command appears on both the red and blue menus.

If these instructions have left you with a lot of questions, don't worry. Each exercise will carefully lead you through the pertinent parts of the program. There is also a *Quick Guide for MicroCase* located inside the front cover of this book. Refer to this guide if you have questions about basic operations in MicroCase.

PART I: *MEASURING CRIME*

Research in criminology is based on three major sources of data. *Official crime rates* are based on crimes reported to or discovered by law enforcement agencies and on arrests. You will become familiar with these crime rates in Exercise 1. *Victimization data* calculate the incidence of crime on the basis of interviews with large national samples during which people are asked about crimes committed against them or members of their household. You will explore some victimization data in Exercise 2. In that exercise you also will examine public opinion on a number of criminal justice issues. Finally, a lot of studies of crime are based on *self-reports*. That is, people are asked whether they have committed various offenses. You will encounter self-report data in Exercise 3. Each kind of data has strengths and weaknesses. Used in conjunction, however, they produce consistent findings.

EXERCISE 1: The Geography of Official Crime Rates

If you have not already done so, start MicroCase according to the instructions in the *Introduction*. With the highlight on **I. Open, Look, Erase or Copy File** *press <ENTER>*. The diskette contains four files, or data sets: **COLLEGEC, FIFTYC, HISCHOOL** and **NORC**. Using the arrow keys to move the highlight, place it on **FIFTYC** and *press <ENTER>*. The screen will tell you that this data file is based on the 50 states and includes 110 variables. *Press <ENTER>* to return to the MENU. *Press <ENTER>* to switch to the **STATISTICAL ANALYSIS MENU**. This menu is red. Place the highlight on **E. Mapping Variables** and *press <ENTER>*. Now the screen asks you for the name or number of the **variable** you wish to map.

A **variable** is anything that varies among the objects being examined. Since we are about to examine the 50 states, let's consider things that vary among them. All 50 states have murders every year, therefore *having* murders *is not* a variable among the 50 states. However, the *number* of murders does vary among the states, and thus the *total* of each state's murders *is* a variable. States also differ in the proportions of their populations who are Hispanic, who play golf, who go to church, or who rob gas stations, and these are also variables. Or, if we are examining individuals rather than states, all traits and characteristics on which people differ — height, weight, political opinions, hobbies, or religion, for example — are variables.

The basic task of social science is to *explain variation*. We do this by trying *to discover connections among variables*. Suppose, for example, that we found that people who differ in terms of their political opinions also differ in terms of their religious affiliation. The next step would be to try to discover *why* these variables are connected.

So, let's look at a variable. Each year the U.S. Department of Justice publishes a volume known as the *Uniform Crime Reports* or as UCR statistics. This thick book contains data on the number of major crimes of various types reported to the police during the previous year. These statistics are gathered from reports submitted to the Federal Bureau of Investigation annually by each of the nation's local police and sheriffs departments. The UCR was first published in 1929 and is the primary source available to criminologists on arrests and on the number of crimes known to the police.

Exercise 1

One of the primary offense categories reported by the UCR is called "larceny-theft." This includes all thefts in which no use of force or fraud was involved. Shoplifting, stripping or breaking into cars, and stealing bicycles are classified as larceny-thefts. Vehicle thefts are not included because these crimes are reported as a separate category, nor are forgery and bad checks classified as larceny-thefts, since each involves fraud. The UCR data also are known as official crime statistics. They have the advantage of having been carefully screened — the police must believe that a crime actually was committed for the report to be counted. They have the disadvantage of being limited to the crimes that are reported to the police or discovered by them. Crimes that go unreported or undiscovered do not show up in these rates. As we will see, sometimes the difference between the official crime rate and the actual rate of offenses is substantial. For example, many people fail to report burglaries, especially when they don't carry insurance. However, criminologists have found the official statistics adequate for many research uses.

CGA Graphics Note

Those of you using newer computers have VGA graphics; those using somewhat older computers will have only CGA or EGA graphics capacity. Because VGA graphics are of much finer resolution, a number of features of the mapping function are available only for VGA computers. MicroCase will check to see which graphics capacity you have and will adjust accordingly.

If you have VGA graphics available on your computer, you will see a menu across the bottom of your screen once the map is completely colored. It will look like this:

Dist   Legnd   Spot   Comp   Name   Print

If this menu does not appear across the bottom of the screen, you will be limited to functions compatible with lower resolution. In the remainder of this introduction to mapping variables, the text will assume you have VGA graphics and that you will be able to use all of the functions shown in this menu. However, for those who do not have VGA graphics, notes will be inserted in the discussion to indicate when a function is not available or to inform you of slight variations in procedures.

To examine the larceny-theft variable *type* **2** and *press* *<ENTER>*.

A map of the United States appears on your screen, and the states appear in five colors from very dark to very light. The darker the state, the greater the number of larceny-thefts that occurred in each state during 1992; the lighter the state, the lower the number of larceny-thefts. The map on your screen will look like this:

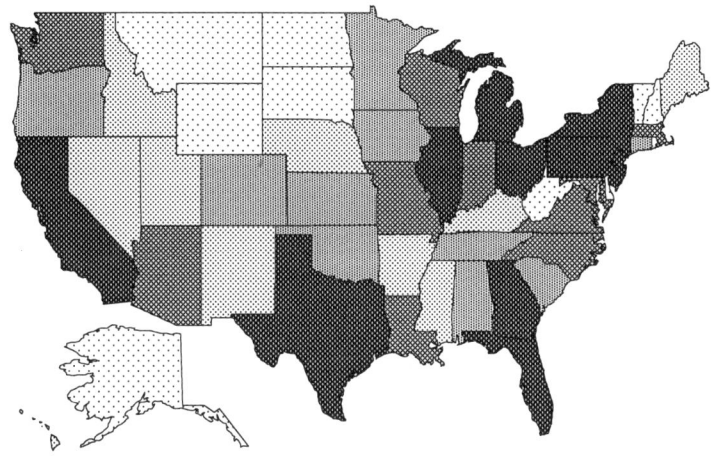

1992: Number of larceny-thefts reported to the police

Now let's see which state was highest. *Type N (for Name)*. One state changes color and is marked by an arrow. In the lower left corner of the screen the name of the indicated state appears, in this case California. Below the name we see that 951,580 larceny-thefts were reported to the police in California during 1992. *Press the down arrow to move to the next highest state*. Now the screen shows us that Texas was second highest with 731,224 and the next highest was Florida with 591,210. If you keep pressing the down arrow you will be able to see the rate for each state as its name appears. However, if you want to see all 50 states ranked from high to low on larceny-thefts, simply *type D (for Distribution)*. Here you can see that Wyoming is in last place — 14,194. If you *press <ENTER>* you will return to the map.

CGA Graphics Note

CGA and **EGA** users: Rather than an arrow appearing on a state, a line will point to the state and the name of the state and its value on a variable will appear at the other end of this line. The commands N (for Name) and D (for Distribution) function in the same way at either level of graphics.

Press <ENTER> twice and the screen asks you the name or number of the next variable you wish to map. This time type **POP 1990** and *press <ENTER>*. (In fact you need only type enough of the variable name to make it unique and the computer will type the rest. So, in this case you could have simply typed **POP 1** and *pressed <ENTER>*.) This map will appear:

Exercise 1

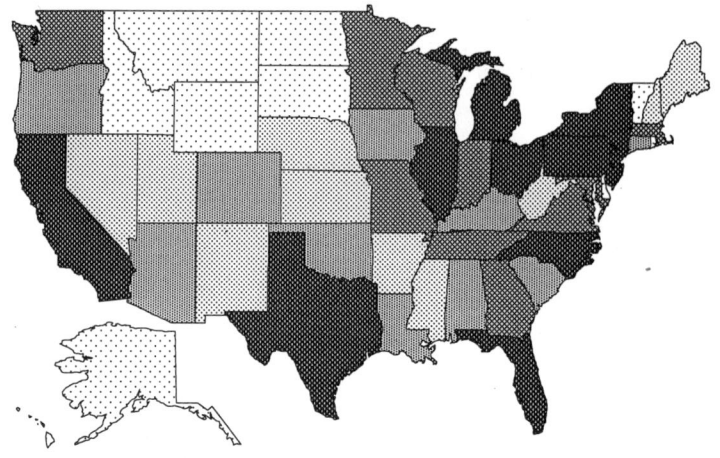

1990: Population in Thousands

This map shows the 1990 population of each state in thousands.

Now let's see which state has the largest population. *Type N (for Name)*. Again a state changes color and is marked by an arrow. The name of this state, California, appears at the lower left of the screen, and below the name we read that the 1990 population was 29,760.0. Keep in mind that this population figure is in thousands so add three zeros to convert it into a total of nearly 30 million. *Press the down arrow to move to the next highest state.* Now the screen shows us that New York has the second largest population — 17,990.5, or nearly 18 million. (In 1994 Texas passed New York to become the second most populous state). To see all 50 states ranked from most to least populous, simply *type D (for Distribution)*. Notice that once again Wyoming is in last place, having the smallest population — 453.6, or less than a half million.

Notice how extremely similar the map of larceny-theft is to this map of total population. That's because all larceny-thefts are committed by people, and where there are more people there are apt to be more thieves. Since California is by far the most populous state, it is not surprising that it is where the most larceny-thefts occur. Nor is it surprising that the fewest larceny-thefts occur in Wyoming, the least populous state.

It is not very interesting to know that some states are larger than others. But, that's about all we can learn from examining raw numbers such as these. However, what we would really like to know is whether people in some states are unusually apt to commit larceny-thefts. That is, are variations in this crime statistic only a reflection of variations in population size, or do other factors enter in? The only way we can pose this question properly is by *removing variations in population size*. What we do is to make each state the same size by converting raw numbers into a **rate**.

A rate is created by reducing the numbers for each unit — in this case, each state — to a common base. Social scientists often use population as their common base. For example, criminologists typically divide the number of reported crimes for each state by its population and then multiply by 100,000. The resulting rate is the number of larceny-thefts per 100,000 population. This rate places California and Wyoming on equal footing. *Press <ENTER> twice.*

Exercise 1

So let's look at a map of the larceny-theft rate per 100,000. But this time, when the screen asks for the name or number of the variable, let's try a third technique for selecting variables. *Press the F3 Key.*

Two windows open on the screen as shown below.

```
 1) CASE ID
 2) #LARCENY
 3) POP 1990
 4) POP GO 90
 5) C.RATE
 6) V.CRIME
 7) P.CRIME
 8) HOMICIDE
 9) RAPE
10) ROBBERY         ┌─────────────────────────────────────────────┐
11) ASSAULT         │ ←: Select/Unselect Variable                 │
12) BURGLARY        │ ↑,↓: PgUp, PgDn, Home, End: Scroll List     │
13) LARCENY         │ →: Examine Variable Description             │
14) AUTO THEFT      │ A: Alphabetic Order                         │
15) HOMICIDE82      │ G: Goto ...                                 │
16) HOMICIDE60      │ S: Search for ...                           │
17) HOMICIDE40      │ Press <ENTER> to Close Window               │
                    └─────────────────────────────────────────────┘
```

The window in the lower right tells you the functions available with this internal codebook feature of MicroCase. The window in the left shows you the name and number of every variable in any given MicroCase data file. Use the *up* and *down arrow keys* to place the highlight on a given variable. The *page up* and *page down keys* will let you move more rapidly up and down the list. The *end key* will take you to the end of the list. The *home key* will take you back to the beginning of the list.

┌───┐
│   │
│   **CGA Graphics Note**   │
│   │
│ **CGA** and **EGA** will have the same capacity as **VGA** users here, except they will not have the second screen at the │
│ lower right telling them the available functions. Other features of the codebook windows outlined below work the │
│ same at both levels of graphics.   │
│   │
└───┘

Now place the highlight on the variable **13) LARCENY** *and press the right arrow key.* An additional window opens as shown below.

```
               ┌───────────────────────────────────────────────────────┐
               │ Minimum:        1611    Maximum:    4434              │
               │ 1992: LARCENIES PER 100,000 (UCR, 93)                 │
 1) CASE ID    │                                                       │
 2) #LARCEN    │                                                       │
 3) POP 1990   │                                                       │
 4) POP GO 90  │                                                       │
 5) C.RATE     │                                                       │
 6) V.CRIME    │                                                       │
 7) P.CRIME    │                                                       │
 8) HOMICIDE   │                                                       │
 9) RAPE       │                                                       │
10) ROBBERY    │   ┌─────────────────────────────────────────────┐     │
11) ASSAULT    │   │ PgUp, PgDn: Move Through Description        │     │
12) BURGLARY   │   │ ↓: Move to Next Variable                    │     │
13) LARCENY    │   │ ↑: Move to Preceding Variable               │     │
14) AUTO THEFT │   │                                             │     │
15) HOMICIDE82 │   │                                             │     │
16) HOMICIDE60 │   │ Press <ENTER> to Close Window               │     │
17) HOMICIDE40 │   └─────────────────────────────────────────────┘     │
               └───────────────────────────────────────────────────────┘
```

Part I - *MEASURING CRIME*

Exercise 1

This window shows you the full description of the variable named **13) LARCENY**. This lets you know that this variable is the larceny-theft rate. To close this window *press <ENTER>*. Now let's try a third way of selecting a variable to be mapped. With the highlight on **13) LARCENY**, *press the left arrow key*. A check mark appears next to the name of the variable which indicates that you have selected it. Now *press <ENTER>*. The map below will appear on your screen.

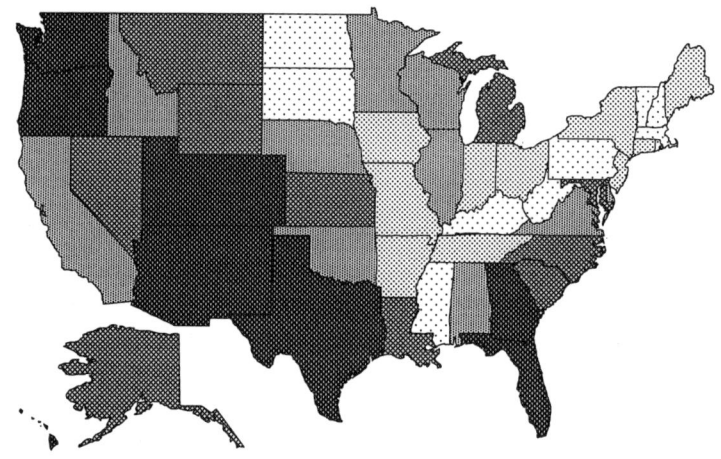

1992: Larcenies per 100,000

This map looks nothing like the two previous maps. *Type N (for Name)*. Again a state changes color, but this time it is Florida, not California. Below the name we see that in 1992 there were 4,434 larceny-thefts for every 100,000 Floridians. *Press the down arrow to move to the next highest state*. Now the screen shows that Hawaii had the second highest larceny-theft rate. To see all 50 states ranked from highest to lowest, simply *type D (for Distribution)*. Notice that Wyoming is no longer last, but is 15th when we examine the rate rather than the number of offenses. Moreover, California and New York are far down the line, while populous Pennsylvania has fallen to 48th place. So, now we know where people are the most and least likely to commit larceny-thefts.

Type S (for Spot). The map changes and a series of spots (or dots) of different sizes and colors appear, one dot for each state. Now, in addition to color differences to indicate which states are higher or lower in larceny-theft rates, the spot for each state is proportional to the value of the variable being mapped. Thus Florida has the largest spot and West Virginia has the smallest. Many people find the spots much easier to interpret than when only color cues are used.

CGA Graphics Note

CGA or **EGA** users will not have the capacity to create spot maps.

Type N (for Name). Now the dot for Florida turns green and the name Florida and the value 4,434 appear in the lower left corner of the screen. Hence, we know that it is highest.

Here too we could use the down arrow to examine all 50 states form highest to lowest. Or *press <ENTER>* to return to the first prompt. We can use the *D (for Distribution)* function to see them all listed from highest to lowest.

Now, map another variable by typing **7** or **P. CRIME** and *pressing <ENTER>*. Or, use the F3 window as explained above.

This variable is based on the total number of serious property crimes reported to the police: burglary, larceny-theft, and motor vehicle theft. These also have been transformed into a rate per 100,000 population.

Anyone who pays attention to crime stories in the national news media "knows" that crime rates are highest in the cities of the Northeast. For example, probably every TV news anchor would agree that compared with New York, New Jersey and Massachusetts, western states such as Arizona, New Mexico, Hawaii and Washington have low crime rates.

However, this map reveals that property crimes are overwhelmingly a western and southern phenomenon. *Type N (for Name)*. Florida has the highest rate — 7,151 offenses per 100,000 residents. *Press the down arrow to move to the next highest state*. Now the screen shows that Arizona has the second highest rate. To see all 50 states ranked from highest to lowest on property crimes, simply *type D (for Distribution)*. Notice that New York is only in 22nd place and New Jersey is in 24th. West Virginia is the lowest with 2,398.

Now map **65** or **COKE USERS**. Use any of the three techniques for selecting a variable. This map will appear:

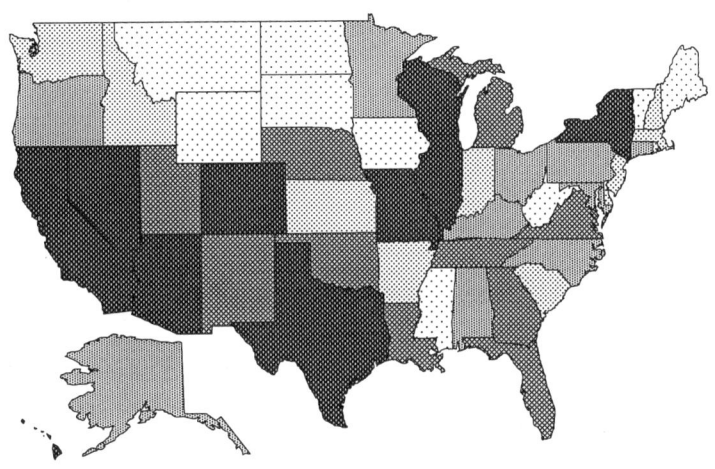

1990: Cocaine addicts per 1,000 population

This variable is based on the estimated number of cocaine addicts per 1,000 population in 1990 as reported by the U.S. Senate Judiciary Committee. When the map is colored in it again reveals a westerly tilt. *Type N (for Name)*. Nevada is number one in terms of its cocaine addiction rate — 24.9 per 1,000 residents. *Press the down arrow to move to the next highest state*. Now the screen shows that New York has the second highest rate — 24.5. To see all 50 states ranked from highest to lowest on cocaine addiction, simply *type D (for Distribution)*. Despite New York being number two, other northeastern states have

Exercise 1

relatively low rates compared with western states such as Arizona, California, Hawaii, Colorado, Texas, and New Mexico.

Now map **8** or **HOMICIDE**. This variable is based on the UCR data — the number of homicides per 100,000 population. When the map is colored in, it again reveals a modestly southern and western tilt. *Type N (for Name)*. Louisiana's homicide rate is 17.4 per 100,000 residents, the highest in the nation. *Press the down arrow to move to the next highest state*. Now the screen shows that New York has the second highest rate (13.2), just ahead of Texas (12.7). To see all 50 states ranked from highest to lowest on homicide, simply *type D (for Distribution)*. Despite New York being number two, once again the other northeastern states have relatively low rates compared with western and southern states.

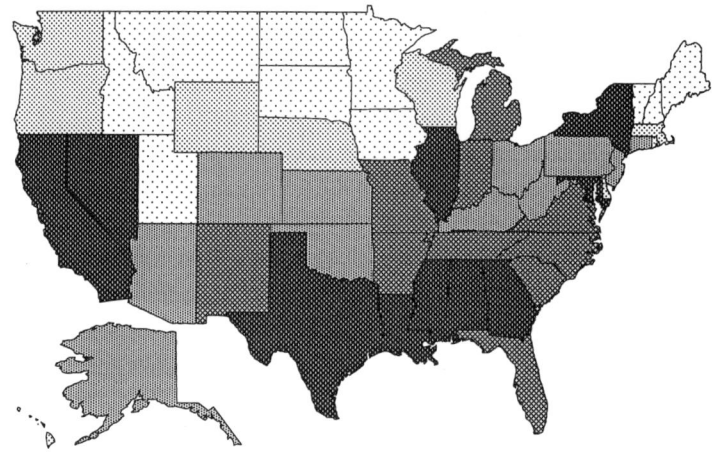

1992: Homicides per 100,000

Now map **51** or **%NO RELIG**. This variable is based on a huge national survey of American adults conducted by Barry A. Kosmin in 1990. In all, 113,000 people were interviewed. Among the questions asked was: "What is your religion?" The map shows the percentage of persons in each state who answered that they had no religion. Percentages are also rates, except they are based on 100 rather than a larger number.

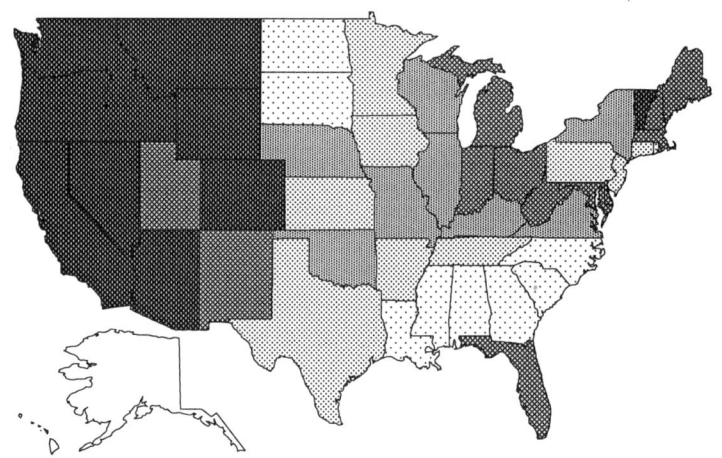

1990: Percent of Population who say they have no religion

Exercise 1

The map shows that having no religion is a *very* western phenomenon. *Type N (for Name)*. We see that 17.2 percent of adults in Oregon have no religion. *Press the down arrow to move to the next highest state*. Now the screen shows that Washington is the second highest state. To see all 50 states ranked from high to low, simply *type D (for Distribution)*. North Dakota is lowest having only 1.6 percent without a religion, closely followed by South Dakota with 2.5 percent.

Notice that Hawaii and Alaska are at the end of the list with values of -99. This is the missing data code, which appears whenever no data are available for a particular case. When Kosmin conducted his poll he did not include Alaska and Hawaii in his sample; that's why we cannot give them a percentage and they remained blank on the map.

Now map **24** or **JAILERS**. Use any of the three techniques for selecting a variable. This map will appear:

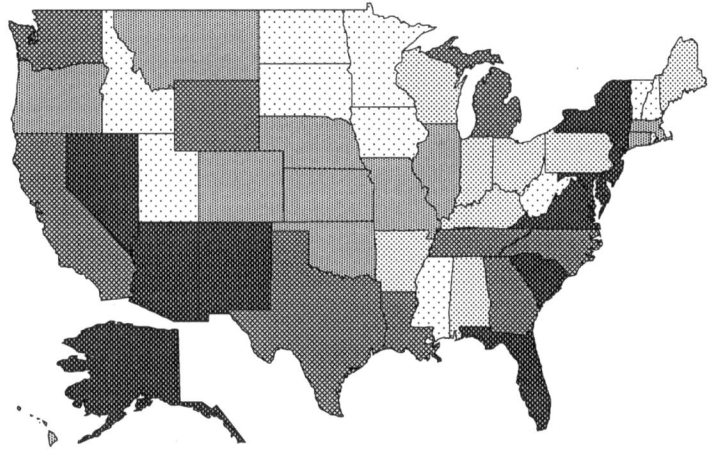

1988: Jail and prison officers per 10,000 population

This variable is the number of jail and prison officers per 10,000 (population).

Type N (for Name). The name New York appears in the lower left corner. Below the name we see that for every 10,000 persons in New York during 1988, there were 29.1 jail and prison officers. *Press the down arrow to move to the next highest state*. Now the screen shows that Florida is the second highest state. To see all 50 states ranked on the jail and prison officers rate, simply *type D (for Distribution)*. West Virginia is lowest having 7.1 jail and prison officers per 10,000, closely followed by North Dakota with 7.2.

CGA Graphics Note

CGA and **EGA** users will not have the following Compare function available. To compare maps you will have to run them one after another and remember how the first one looks. This is less efficient than using the compare feature, but students using the first and second editions of the lab book found no difficulty in doing the assigned comparisons without the compare function.

Part I - *MEASURING CRIME*

Exercise 1

Press <ENTER> to return to the map. Then *type C (for Compare)*. Now the map shrinks to half size and moves to the top of the screen. The screen asks for the name or number of the variable for comparison. Type **49** or **%DROPOUTS** and *press <ENTER>*. A second map will appear.

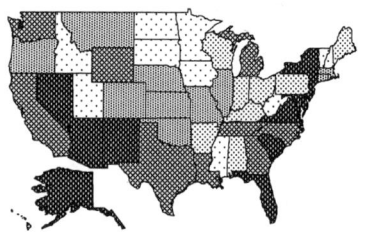

1988: JAIL AND PRISON OFFICERS PER 10,000 POPULATION (S.A., 1991)

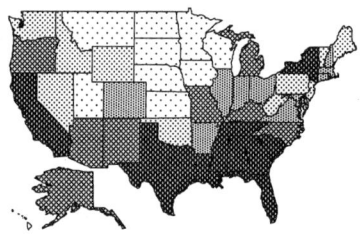

1990: PERCENT OF PERSONS WHO LEFT SCHOOL WITHOUT GRADUATING FROM HIGH SCHOOL (WA, 1993)

The second map shows the percent of students who quit without graduating from high school. The two maps are quite similar — suggesting that more jail and prison guards are required in states with higher dropout rates.

To clear the lower map, *press <ENTER>*. Again the screen asks for the name or number of the variable you wish to use for comparison. Use **23** or **COPS** and *press <ENTER>*.

This maps shows the number of state and local law enforcement officers per 10,000. These two maps also look alike.

Press <ENTER> twice to return to the full-size map of **JAILERS**. Now *press S* (for Spot). Then *type C (for Compare)*. Now the map of dots shrinks to half size and moves to the top of the screen. The screen asks for the name or number of the variable for comparison. Type **61** or **HUNTING** and *press <ENTER>*. A second map will appear.

This map shows the percentage of residents of each state who purchased hunting licenses. The maps do *not* look alike. In fact, they are almost the reverse of one another.

Now, it's your turn to examine and compare some maps.

Name: _____   ***Worksheets*** - Exercise 1

> *Workbook exercises and software are copyrighted. Copying is prohibited by law.*

1. *Open* the **FIFTYC** data file and select the mapping function. Map variable **8** or **HOMICIDE.**

    Write in the caption of the map: _____
    _____

    Use the Compare map function and use **16** or **HOMICIDE60** as the second map.

    Write in the caption of the map: _____
    _____

    Would you say these two maps are (circle one):   Very Similar
                                                       Somewhat Similar
                                                       Not Very Similar

    Press <ENTER> to clear the second map and select a new second map: **17** or **HOMICIDE40** as the second map.

    Write in the caption of the map: _____
    _____

    Would you say these two maps are (circle one):   Very Similar
                                                       Somewhat Similar
                                                       Not Very Similar

2. Return to the beginning of the task and Map variable **9** or **RAPE**.

    Write in the caption of the map: _____
    _____

    List the three highest states: 1 _____

                                     2 _____

                                     3 _____

Part I - *MEASURING CRIME*   *13.*

Worksheets - Exercise 1

List the three lowest states:

48 _____

49 _____

50 _____

Use the **C**ompare map function and use **16** or **HOMICIDE60** as the second map.

Write in the caption of the map: _____

_____

Would you say these two maps are **(circle one)**:　　　　　　　Very Similar
　　　　　　　　　　　　　　　　　　　　　　　　　　　　Somewhat Similar
　　　　　　　　　　　　　　　　　　　　　　　　　　　　Not Very Similar

Press <ENTER> to clear the second map and select a new second map: **51** or **% NO RELIG.** as the second map.

Write in the caption of the map: _____

_____

Would you say these two maps are **(circle one)**:　　　　　　　Very Similar
　　　　　　　　　　　　　　　　　　　　　　　　　　　　Somewhat Similar
　　　　　　　　　　　　　　　　　　　　　　　　　　　　Not Very Similar

Press <ENTER> to clear the second map and select a new second map: **50** or **ABORTION** as the second map.

Write in the caption of the map: _____

_____

Would you say these two maps are **(circle one)**:　　　　　　　Very Similar
　　　　　　　　　　　　　　　　　　　　　　　　　　　　Somewhat Similar
　　　　　　　　　　　　　　　　　　　　　　　　　　　　Not Very Similar

Which of these three comparisons did you find the most surprising or interesting? Explain.

Name: _____ ***Worksheets*** - Exercise 1

3. Return to the beginning of the task and Map variable **10** or **ROBBERY**.

   Write in the caption of the map: _____
   _____

   List the three highest states: 1 _____

   2 _____

   3 _____

   List the three lowest states: 48 _____

   49 _____

   50 _____

   Use the **C**ompare map function and use **61** or **HUNTING** as the second map.

   Write in the caption of the map: _____
   _____

Would you say these two maps are **(circle one)**:   Very Similar
                                                        Somewhat Similar
                                                        Not Very Similar

Press <ENTER> to clear the second map and select a new second map: **26** or **% METROPOL** as the second map.

   Write in the caption of the map: _____
   _____

Would you say these two maps are **(circle one)**:   Very Similar
                                                        Somewhat Similar
                                                        Not Very Similar

Part I - *MEASURING CRIME*   15.

Worksheets - Exercise 1

Which of these comparisons did you find the most surprising or interesting? Explain.

4. Return to the beginning of the task and Map variable **11** or **ASSAULT**.

    Write in the caption of the map: _____

    _____

    List the three highest states: 1 _____

    2 _____

    3 _____

    List the three lowest states: 48 _____

    49 _____

    50 _____

    Use the **Compare** map function and use **8** or **HOMICIDE** as the second map.

    Write in the caption of the map: _____

    _____

    Would you say these two maps are **(circle one)**:   Very Similar
    Somewhat Similar
    Not Very Similar

    Press <ENTER> to clear the second map and select a new second map: **57** or **TV DISHES** as the second map.

    Write in the caption of the map: _____

    _____

16.   CRIMINOLOGY - *An Introduction Using MicroCase*

Name: _____   ***Worksheets*** - Exercise 1

Would you say these two maps are (circle one):   Very Similar
                                                              Somewhat Similar
                                                                Not Very Similar

Press <ENTER> to clear the second map and select a new second map: **67** or **LIQUOR** as the second map.

   Write in the caption of the map: _____

   _____

Would you say these two maps are (circle one):   Very Similar
                                                              Somewhat Similar
                                                                Not Very Similar

Which of these three comparisons did you find the most surprising or interesting? Explain.

5. Return to the beginning of the task and Map variable **44** or **MALE HOMES**.

    Write in the caption of the map: _____

    _____

    List the three highest states: 1 _____

                                        2 _____

                                        3 _____

Part I - *MEASURING CRIME*   17.

Worksheets - Exercise 1

List the three lowest states:

48 _____

49 _____

50 _____

Use the **C**ompare map function and use **56** or **PLAYBOY** as the second map.

Would you say these two maps are (circle one):

Very Similar
Somewhat Similar
Not Very Similar

Press <ENTER> to clear the second map and select a new second map: **67** or **LIQUOR** as the second map.

Write in the caption of the map: _____

_____

Would you say these two maps are (circle one):

Very Similar
Somewhat Similar
Not Very Similar

Which of these comparisons did you find the most surprising or interesting? Explain.

CRIMINOLOGY - *An Introduction Using MicroCase*

EXERCISE 2: Victimization and Public Opinion

In addition to analyzing data based on official police statistics, criminologists often examine surveys of the population which ask people whether they have been the *victims* of various kinds of crime. One purpose of such victimization studies is to make up for the underreporting that occurs in the official statistics. Presumably, even people who failed to call the police about a crime will mention it to an interviewer when asked to do so. The weakness of victimization data is that many crimes are sufficiently rare so that huge samples are needed in order to get even a few victims of such crimes. For example, based on the official rape rate for 1990 we could expect only 11 rape victims to turn up in a sample including 3,000 Americans. Even if the actual rate of rape is twice the official rate, only 22 victims could turn up in such a sample. No useful conclusions can be drawn from so few victims. And, of course, murder victims can't be interviewed at all. However, in conjunction with the official statistics, victimization studies help form a fuller picture of crime.

In this exercise you will begin to explore victimization data. In addition, you will examine public opinion on criminal justice issues.

Start MicroCase according to the instructions in the *Introduction*. With the highlight on **I. Open, Look, Erase or Copy File** *press <ENTER>*. The diskette contains four files, or data sets. Using the arrow keys to move the highlight, place it on **NORC** and *press <ENTER>*. The screen will tell you that this data file is based on the combined 1990, 1991 and 1993 General Social Surveys, which consist of a national sample of 4,495 Americans age 18 and over. Thirty-six variables from this survey are included here. *Press <ENTER>* to return to the MENU. *Press <ENTER>* to switch to the **STATISTICAL ANALYSIS MENU**. This menu is red. Place the highlight on **A. Univariate Statistics** and *press <ENTER>* or just *type* **A**. Now the screen asks you for the name or number of the variable you wish to examine. *Type* **21** and *press <ENTER>*. *Press <ENTER>* again to skip the subset variable option. This pie chart will appear:

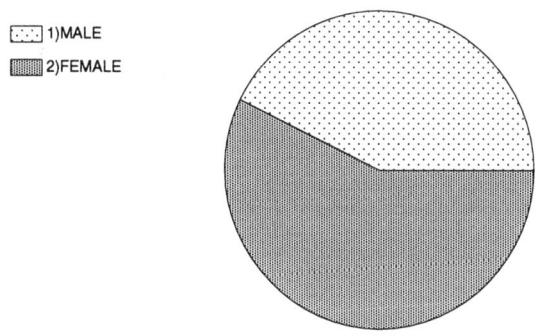

As you can see, women outnumber men in the sample. *Type D (for Distribution).* (**If you have only CGA graphics**, *press T for Table*.) This screen will appear:

Part I - *MEASURING CRIME* 19.

Exercise 2

RESPONDENT'S SEX

MALE	1925	42.8%
FEMALE	2570	57.2%

Look at the first column of figures, which shows the frequencies or actual numbers. Here we see that there are 1925 males in this sample and 2570 females, for a total of 4495. Frequencies often are a bit hard to interpret, so the second column of figures shows the percentages of males and females — 42.8 percent are men and 57.2 percent are women. There should be more women than men in the sample because there are more women than men in the population age 18 and over. This is because the average woman outlives the average man by nearly seven years.

However, the sample isn't absolutely correct. The census reports that for 1990, only 54 percent, not 57 percent, of the population 18 and over were women. Part of the difference is that surveys *always overestimate* the percent female in the population. One reason is that far more men than women are transients lacking a permanent residence where they can be found by survey interviewers. Another reason is that men are far more likely than women to be in prisons and jails and among other institutionalized populations which are not included in most surveys. But some part of the difference we have found here probably is due to random fluctuations.

It is possible to base research on data gathered from a random *sample* of a population, rather than to gather data on *everyone*, because we can calculate the odds that persons included in the sample will be like those not included. That is, if we randomly select people from a population, as our sample grows in size it will come ever closer to matching the characteristics of the population from which it is selected. You may have noticed that stories in the press based on surveys sometimes mention that the results are accurate within a particular percentage range — plus or minus 3 percentage points is a common range. For a sample of any given size, we can compute the probable range of accuracy of estimates based on the sample. With samples the size of this one, our estimate of the percentage of females in the population should be accurate within 1.6 percentage points, plus or minus. That is, if our sample tells us that the population is 57 percent women, 95 percent of the time the actual percentage in the population will be somewhere between 55.4 and 58.6 percent. This range is referred to as the **confidence interval**.

Press <ENTER> twice to return to the first prompt and select variable **1** or **FEAR WALK** as the next variable. Keep in mind that you can select a variable by number, by name, or through the F3 window. *Press <ENTER>* to skip the next option. After the pie chart appears, *type D*. These data will appear:

Is there any area right around here — that is, within a mile — where you would be afraid to walk alone at night?

	Frequency	%
YES	1261	42.7
NO	1695	57.3

Four Americans in 10 say they would be afraid to walk around in their neighborhood at night. Perhaps this next variable will tell us a bit about why so many people are frightened.

Press <ENTER> twice to clear the screen and select variable **4** or **KNOW MURD.** as the next variable. After the pie chart appears, *type D*. These data will appear:

Within the past 12 months, how many people have you known personally that were victims of homicide?

	Frequency	%
NONE	1244	90.8
ONE	81	5.9
2 OR MORE	45	3.3

Nearly 1 American out of 10 claimed to know someone personally who had been murdered during the past year. Notice that the total number of cases here is smaller than on some other variables. That is because this item was asked only in the 1990 survey. Some other items we also will examine were asked only of randomly selected subsets of each survey.

Next, let's see the univariate distribution of variable **2** or **BURGLED?**. After the pie chart appears, *type D*. These data will appear:

During the last year — that is, between March and now — did anyone break into or somehow illegally get into your (apartment/home)?

	Frequency	%
YES	171	5.7
NO	2803	94.3

About 6 percent of Americans reported that they had been burglarized during the past year. According to the official crime report data (UCR), only 3.5 percent of all households were broken into during 1990. The difference between the two percentages is easily understood. First of all, many people fail to report a minor burglary to the police, but will do so when asked directly about it. Second, many people do not report even serious burglaries if they are not covered by insurance, since they know they are not likely to recover any of their property. Third, people in areas with the highest burglary rates often do not trust the police or wish to call attention to themselves.

These points are confirmed by the 1990 National Crime Survey (NCS). Based on 60,000 American households, this huge victimization study is conducted periodically by the Bureau of the Census and the Bureau of Justice Statistics. For 1990, the NCS reported that 5.4 percent of households had been burglarized, almost identical with these findings from the

Exercise 2

General Social Surveys. The tiny difference between the two estimates is the result of random error.

You may wonder why you are not using the NCS data rather than data from the smaller GSS sample. First of all, even MicroCase couldn't pack a huge 60,000 household sample on a diskette. Second, while the NCS data yield more reliable rates, they are very deficient in other data about their respondents, having no data on attitudes, beliefs, or social behavior.

Now, let's see the univariate distribution of variable **3** or **ROBBED?**. After the pie chart appears, *type D*. These data will appear:

During the last year, did anyone take something directly from you by using force — such as a stickup, mugging, or threat?

	Frequency	%
YES	58	2.0
NO	2916	98.0

Here we see a characteristic problem of victimization research — robbery is such a relatively rare event that only 58 people reported having been victims of this crime. Even in the NCS, too few robbery victims turn up to provide a basis for much analysis.

In any event, these data suggest that 2.0 percent of Americans are being robbed yearly. The UCR data reported that 0.3 percent of Americans were robbed in 1992. The difference probably involves both underreporting to the police and random error in the sample estimate.

Because of their large samples, the National Crime Surveys surpass the General Social Surveys in terms of statistical accuracy. But as mentioned, the shortcoming of these huge studies is that they include very little other information about their respondents. We don't know which respondents hang out in bars, own guns, or attend church regularly. Nor can we seek links between being a crime victim and people's opinions about criminal justice issues such as police use of force, belief in capital punishment, or support for gun control legislation.

In the remainder of this exercise you will explore some of these aspects of the General Social Surveys.

Let's begin with variable **11** or **GO TO BARS**. After the pie chart appears, *type D*. These data will appear:

How often do you go to a bar or tavern?

	Frequency	%
WEEKLY	260	8.6
SOMETIMES	1184	39.2
NEVER	1574	52.2

The majority of Americans report that they never go to a bar or tavern.

Try another: variable **5** or **COPS HIT?**. After the pie chart appears, *type D*. These data will appear:

Are there any situations you can imagine in which you would approve of a policeman striking an adult male citizen?

	Frequency	%
YES	2048	72.9
NO	761	27.1

Most Americans accept the idea that the police may find it necessary to hit people in some situations. Perhaps it is more interesting that 1 in 4 does not.

Now, it's your turn.

Name: _____   **Worksheets** - Exercise 2

> *Workbook exercises and software are copyrighted. Copying is prohibited by law.*

1. *Open* the **NORC** data file and select the Univariate Statistics function. Select **7** or **EXECUTE?** as the variable. After the pie chart appears, *type D*.

   Write in the question: _____

   _____

   _____

   Now, fill in the appropriate numbers.

		Frequency	%
1.	FAVOR	_____	_____
2.	OPPOSE	_____	_____

   How would you answer this question? **(circle one)**   1   2

2. Select **6** or **COURTS?** as the variable. After the pie chart appears, *type D*.

   Write in the question: _____

   _____

   _____

   Now, fill in the appropriate numbers.

		Frequency	%
1.	TOO HARSH	_____	_____
2.	NOT ENOUGH	_____	_____
3.	ABOUT RIGH*	_____	_____

   How would you answer this question? **(circle one)**   1   2   3

* Since MicroCase limits variable names and categories to 10 characters, some variable information is purposely shortened or misspelled. To be consistent with the software, generally the same spelling is used in the text whenever variable names or categories are referred to.

Part I - *MEASURING CRIME*

Worksheets - Exercise 2

3. Select **14** or **GUN LAW?** as the variable. After the pie chart appears, *type D*.

   Write in the question: _____

   _____

   _____

   Now, fill in the appropriate numbers.

	Frequency	%
1. FAVOR	_____	_____
2. OPPOSE	_____	_____

   How would you answer this question? (circle one)   1   2

4. Select **15** or **OWN GUN?** as the variable. After the pie chart appears, *type D*.

   Write in the question: _____

   _____

   _____

   Now, fill in the appropriate numbers.

	Frequency	%
1. YES	_____	_____
2. NO	_____	_____

   How would you answer this question? (circle one)   1   2

Name: _____   ***Worksheets*** - Exercise 2

5. Select **16** or **HUNT?** as the variable. After the pie chart appears, *type D*.

   Write in the question: _____

   _____

   _____

   Now, fill in the appropriate numbers.

	Frequency	%
1. HUNTS	_____	_____
2. NOT HUNTS	_____	_____

   How would you answer this question? **(circle one)**   1   2

6. Select **8** or **CRIME $** as the variable. After the pie chart appears, *type D*.

   Write in the question: _____

   _____

   _____

   Now, fill in the appropriate numbers.

	Frequency	%
1. TOO LITTLE	_____	_____
2. RIGHT	_____	_____
3. TOO MUCH	_____	_____

   How would you answer this question? **(circle one)**   1   2   3

Part I - *MEASURING CRIME*

Worksheets - Exercise 2

7. Select **9** or **DRUGS $** as the variable. After the pie chart appears, *type D*.

   Write in the question: _____

   _____

   _____

   Now, fill in the appropriate numbers.

	Frequency	%
1. TOO LITTLE	_____	_____
2. RIGHT	_____	_____
3. TOO MUCH	_____	_____

   How would you answer this question? **(circle one)**   1   2   3

8. Select **10** or **GRASS?** as the variable. After the pie chart appears, *type D*.

   Write in the question: _____

   _____

   _____

   Now, fill in the appropriate numbers.

	Frequency	%
1. SHOULD	_____	_____
2. SHOULDN'T	_____	_____

   How would you answer this question? **(circle one)**   1   2

28. CRIMINOLOGY - *An Introduction Using MicroCase*

Name: _____ ***Worksheets*** - Exercise 2

9. Select **12** or **DRINK?** as the variable. After the pie chart appears, *type D*.

   Write in the question: _____
   _____
   _____

   Now, fill in the appropriate numbers.

	Frequency	%
1. DRINKS	_____	_____
2. ABSTAINS	_____	_____

   How would you answer this question? **(circle one)**   1   2

10. Select **13** or **DRUNK** as the variable. After the pie chart appears, *type D*.

    Write in the question: _____
    _____
    _____

    Now, fill in the appropriate numbers.

	Frequency	%
1. GETS DRUNK	_____	_____
2. NO	_____	_____
3. ABSTAINS	_____	_____

    How would you answer this question? **(circle one)**   1   2   3

Part I - *MEASURING CRIME*

Worksheets - Exercise 2

11. Select **34** or **HAPPY?** as the variable. After the pie chart appears, *type D*.

    Write in the question: _____

    _____

    _____

    Now, fill in the appropriate numbers.

	Frequency	%
1. VERY HAPPY	_____	_____
2. PRETTY HAPPY	_____	_____
3. NOT TOO	_____	_____

    How would you answer this question? **(circle one)**   1   2   3

12. Looking back over these worksheets, select the question that most interested or surprised you in terms of how people responded, and explain your reaction to it.

CRIMINOLOGY - *An Introduction Using MicroCase*

EXERCISE 3: Self-Report Data: Student Samples

In this exercise we are going to examine self-report data from two questionnaire studies. The first consists of a large, nationwide survey of high school seniors — 11,995 in all. The survey was part of an elaborate study of students conducted during the late 1980s for the U.S. Department of Education by the Survey Research Center, University of Michigan. The second data file consists of 542 students attending a large university, who filled out questionnaires in 1993. The results of this college-student survey are very similar to results obtained at many other schools. But, because the data reveal rather high levels of involvement in crime and in illegal alcohol and drug use, it would be unfair to identify the school and subject it to unjustified bad publicity.

Because the sample of high school seniors is so large it yields very accurate statistics, but it also will take a bit longer for MicroCase to put the results on the screen as compared with the far smaller sample of college students.

Start MicroCase according to the instructions in the *Introduction* and *open* the **HISCHOOL** data set. On the red **STATISTICAL ANALYSIS MENU**, place the highlight on **A. Univariate Statistics** and *press <ENTER>* (or just *type* **A**). Now the screen asks you for the name or number of the variable you wish to examine. *Type* **1** or **LAW TROUBL** and *press <ENTER> twice*. This pie chart will appear.

I have been in serious trouble with the law

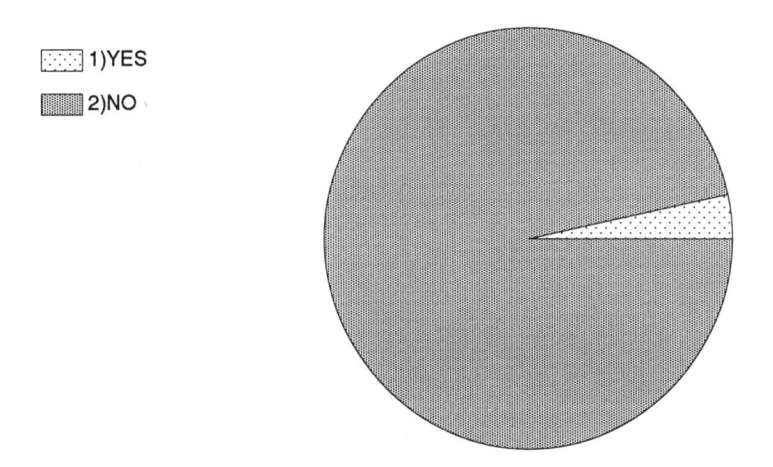

1) YES
2) NO

As you can see, few students have been in serious trouble with the law. Keep in mind, however, that many more of these students will have been picked up by the police for various reasons, but the results did not cause them to define it as having been in "serious trouble." So what we have here are those who were accused of doing something carrying a significant penalty.

Type D (for Distribution) (or if you have only CGA graphics *type T for Table*) and the screen will show you the frequency and the percentage of those who said yes or no to this question.

Exercise 3

	Frequency	%
YES	405	3.7
NO	10672	96.3

Altogether 405 of these high school seniors reported having been in serious trouble with the law — or 3.7 percent. Of course, this does not tell us how many students have broken various laws, only the number who have been caught. However, people who engage in serious offenses tend to be repeat offenders who eventually get caught, so this item does identify the worst offenders in this group (or at least most of them) and will allow us to assess *who* engages in juvenile crime.

There is, of course, concern whether self-report data are reliable. Just as official crime statistics underestimate crime because of crimes that go unreported, some people probably fail to admit that they have been in trouble with the police, shoplifted, used drugs, or whatever, when asked about their behavior via questionnaires or interviews. Consequently, through the years a good deal of research has been done to check the accuracy of self-report data — will people be truthful? Some of these studies compared teenagers' self-reports of delinquent behavior against police records, re-interviewed a sample of respondents using a lie detector, and checked the answers given by some respondents against reports about their behavior given by their friends. The results show that there is in fact a bit of under-reporting, but far less than expected. Therefore self-report data are sufficiently trustworthy for research. Moreover, the results also show that people are more truthful when responding to a self-administered questionnaire than when answering an interviewer — both of these studies of students were based on questionnaires.

Press <ENTER> twice to clear the screen and select **3** or **DRINK/30** as the next variable.

On how many occasions (if any) have you had alcohol to drink (beer, wine, liquor) during the past thirty days?

After the pie chart appears, *type D*. These data will appear:

	Frequency	%
NEVER	3033	28.9
1 OR 2	3016	28.7
3 OR MORE	4452	42.4

About three out of four high school seniors had drunk alcohol during the past month and nearly half had done so three or more times. As minors, all who drank broke the law.

Press <ENTER> twice to clear the screen and select **4** or **MARIJUANA** as the next variable.

On how many occasions (if any) have you used HASHISH (hash) or MARIJUANA (grass, pot, dope)?

After the pie chart appears, *type D*. These data will appear:

	Frequency	%
NEVER	4971	50.2
1 OR 2	1111	11.2
SOMETIMES	1696	17.1
OFTEN	2130	21.5

Half of high school seniors reported they had used marijuana or hashish at least once, and more than a third reported using it a number of times — one out of five said "often."

Now let's see how college students responded when they were asked some questions about their illegal behavior. The strength of self-report data is that they allow us to examine characteristics of *all* offenders, not just of persons who have gotten into serious trouble with the police. In general, the results of these studies justify the use of the self-report method.

Return to the main menu and *open* the **COLLEGEC** data set. On the red **STATISTICAL ANALYSIS MENU**, place the highlight on **A. Univariate Statistics** and *press <ENTER>* (or just type **A**). Now the screen asks you for the name or number of the variable you wish to examine. *Type* **1** or **TICKET?** and *press <ENTER>* twice. After the pie chart appears, *type D*. These data will appear:

Have you ever received a ticket, or been charged by the police, for a traffic violation — other than illegal parking?

	Frequency	%
YES	288	53.6
NO	249	46.4

Slightly more than half of these college students admitted having been ticketed for a traffic violation. However, the criminologists who designed this question (it is widely used) weren't all that interested in traffic violations. Instead, they used this question as a filter for the next question.

Press <ENTER> twice to clear the screen and select variable **2** or **PICKED UP?** as the next variable. After the pie chart appears, *type D*. These data will appear.

Exercise 3

Were you ever picked up, or charged, by the police for any other reason, whether or not you were guilty?

	Frequency	%
PICKED UP	118	22.0
NOT	419	78.0

About one of five of these college students admit to having been picked up by the police. Although we don't know what they got picked up for, we do know that they aren't reporting traffic stops or drunk driving. Although this might strike you as rather high for students at a good university, it is typical for college students around the nation. Moreover, college students are about as likely to report having been picked up by the police as are *all* Americans of college age. When precisely this same question was asked by the GSS in 1984 (the most recent year available), 24 percent of persons age 18 through 23 said they had been picked up.

Now, it's your turn to examine self-report data based on college students. You also will be asked to compare the results with what you think a similar survey might find at your own college or university.

Name: _____   *Worksheets* - Exercise 3

Workbook exercises and software are copyrighted. Copying is prohibited by law.

---

1. *Open* the **COLLEGEC** data file and select the Univariate Statistics function. Select **3** or **SHOPLIFT** as the variable. After the pie chart appears, *type D.*

    Write in the question: _____
    _____

    Now, fill in the appropriate numbers.

	Frequency	%
YES	_____	_____
NO	_____	_____

    Suppose students at your school were asked this question.
    Do you think they would be similar to these students? **(circle one)**   SIMILAR
    　　　　　　　　　　　　　　　　　　　　　　　　　　　　　　　　　　　　LESS SHOPLIFT HERE
    　　　　　　　　　　　　　　　　　　　　　　　　　　　　　　　　　　　MORE SHOPLIFTING HERE

2. Select **4** or **DRINK?** as the variable. After the pie chart appears, *type D.*

    Write in the question: _____
    _____
    _____

    Now, fill in the appropriate numbers.

	Frequency	%
DRINK NOW	_____	_____
ABSTAIN	_____	_____

3. Select **5** or **THROW UP?** as the variable. After the pie chart appears, *type D.*

    Write in the question: _____
    _____
    _____

Part I - *MEASURING CRIME*

Worksheets - Exercise 3

Now, fill in the appropriate numbers.

	Frequency	%
THROW UP	_____	_____
NO	_____	_____

Suppose students at your school were asked these two questions.
Do you think they would be similar to these students? **(circle one)**   SIMILAR
                                                                          LESS DRINKING HERE
                                                                          MORE DRINKING HERE

4. Select **6** or **POT NOW** as the variable. After the pie chart appears, *type D*.

   Write in the question: _____

   _____

   _____

   Now, fill in the appropriate numbers.

	Frequency	%
PAST YEAR	_____	_____
NO	_____	_____

   Suppose students at your school were asked this question.
   Do you think they would be similar to these students? **(circle one)**   SIMILAR
                                                                             LESS USE HERE
                                                                             MORE USE HERE

5. Select **7** or **COKE NOW** as the variable. After the pie chart appears, *type D*.

   Write in the question: _____

   _____

   _____

36.   CRIMINOLOGY - *An Introduction Using MicroCase*

| Name: | ***Worksheets*** - Exercise 3 |

Now, fill in the appropriate numbers.

	Frequency	%
PAST YEAR	_____	_____
NO	_____	_____

Suppose students at your school were asked this question.
Do you think they would be similar to these students? (circle one)   SIMILAR
    LESS USE HERE
    MORE USE HERE

6. Select **14** or **STUDY TIME** as the variable. After the pie chart appears, *type D*.

   Write in the question: _____

   _____

   _____

Now, fill in the appropriate numbers.

	Frequency	%
UNDER 10	_____	_____
10-14	_____	_____
15-20	_____	_____
OVER 20	_____	_____

Suppose students at your school were asked this question.
Do you think they would be similar to these students? (circle one)   SIMILAR
    LESS STUDY HERE
    MORE STUDY HERE

7. Select **17** or **OWN CAR?** as the variable. After the pie chart appears, *type D*.

   Write in the question: _____

   _____

   _____

Part I - *MEASURING CRIME*

Worksheets - Exercise 3

Now, fill in the appropriate numbers.

	Frequency	%
YES	_____	_____
NO	_____	_____

Suppose students at your school were asked this question.
Do you think they would be similar to these students? **(circle one)**   SIMILAR
                                                                           FEWER CARS HERE
                                                                           MORE CARS HERE

8. On the basis of all these results, discuss the following claim: Crime, alcohol and drug abuse primarily are the result of poverty and the lack of hope — they are concentrated among the uneducated, especially school dropouts, who have little hope for a better life.

PART II: *ANALYZING CRIME DATA*

Exercise 1 pointed out that the basic task of social science is to *explain variation*. In the first three exercises you examined a lot of variation: Some people are afraid to walk around their neighborhoods at night, others aren't; some people have been burglarized, some haven't; some states have high homicide rates, some don't. In the next exercises, you will begin to investigate such variations. For example, you will try to discover *who* is afraid to walk around at night and *why*.

EXERCISE 4: Fear of Violence: Cross-Tabulation

Open the **NORC** *data set* and switch to the **STATISTICAL ANALYSIS MENU**. This menu is red. Place the highlight on **B. Tabular Statistics** and *press <ENTER>* (or just *type* **B**).

When the screen asks for the name or number of the row variable, *type* **1** or **FEAR WALK** or use the F3 window to select this variable. When the screen asks for the name or number of the column variable, *type* **36** or **SINGLE/MAR**. When the screen asks for a control variable, simply *press <ENTER>*. When it asks for a subset variable, simply *press <ENTER>*.

You are about to test this hypothesis: **Single people are more likely to be afraid to walk around in their neighborhood at night**.

This table is now on your screen:

	SINGLE	MARRIED
YES	261	576
NO	348	968
TOTAL	609	1544

Across the top are the labels: SINGLE and MARRIED. All persons who said they had never been married are in the column labeled single, and all who currently were married are in the column labeled married — widowed and divorced people are not included in the table. Down the side of the table are the answers given by each respondent to the question of whether or not they were afraid to walk in their neighborhood at night. The numbers within the table reflect the numbers of who said yes or no. The question was asked only of a random subset of respondents, hence 1539 are classified as missing.

Looking at the table we see that of the 609 who have never been married, 261 said they feared to walk at night and 348 said they would not. Looking at the next column of the table we see that there were a lot more married people who said yes — 576. But there also

Exercise 4

were many more married people who said no — 968. That's because there are many more respondents who are married than who have not married.

This makes it obvious that we can't simply compare raw numbers of respondents. We must take differences in the size of populations into account. To do so, we can calculate the **percentage** who said yes and no in each group. To do that, simply *press C for column percentages*. The screen adds percentages to the table:

	SINGLE	MARRIED
YES	42.9	37.3
NO	57.1	62.7
TOTAL	100.0	100.0

These data show that, as predicted, single people *are* more likely than married people to say they would be afraid to walk in their neighborhood at night — perhaps because they are less likely to live in suburban neighborhoods. To see that single people are more apt to be afraid, read the table from left to right just as you read ordinary text, and compare percentages. Thus, 42.9 percent of single people said yes, while 37.3 percent of married respondents did so. Or, comparing across the lower row of the table, we can see that 57.1 percent of single people said they would not be afraid compared with 62.7 of married people.

Clearly our hypothesis is supported by the data — at least slightly. But, before we rush out to tell the world that single people are more apt to be afraid of crime than are married people, we must notice that the difference is rather small. Small differences raise questions for survey data analysis.

As noted in Exercise 2, **random sampling** is the basis of all survey research. Rather than interview all members of a population, survey researchers interview only a sample. As long as this sample is selected randomly, so that all members have an equal chance of being selected, the results based on the sample can be generalized to the entire population. That is, the laws of probability allow us to **calculate the odds** that something observed in the sample accurately reflects a feature of the population sampled — subject to **two limitations**.

First of all, the sample must be sufficiently **large**. Obviously, we couldn't use a sample of two people as the basis for describing the American population — there is a very high probability that they would both be white, for example. For this reason, survey studies include enough cases so that they can accurately reflect the population in terms of variations in such characteristics as age, sex, education, religion, and the like. The accuracy of a sample is a function of its size. The larger the sample, the more accurate it is. Good survey studies are based on 1,000 cases or more — this sample is based on 4,495 Americans, and the random sub-sample who were asked this question included 2,153 respondents.

The second limitation has to do with the **magnitude (or size) of the difference** observed in a table. Because samples are based on the principle of random selection, they are subject to some degree of random fluctuation. That is, for purely random reasons there can be small differences between the sample and the population. Thus whenever we examine cross-tabulations such as those shown above, social scientists always must ask whether what they are seeing is a real difference, one that would turn up if the entire population were examined, or only a random fluctuation, which does not reflect a true difference in the population.

The small size of the difference observed above (on a sample this size) will always make an experienced analyst suspicious that it is merely the result of random fluctuations.

Fortunately, there is a simple technique for calculating the odds that a given difference is real or random. This calculation is called a **test of statistical significance.** Differences observed in samples are said to be statistically significant when the *odds against* random results are high enough. There is no mathematical way to determine just how high is high enough. But, through the years social scientists have settled on the rule of thumb that they will ignore all differences unless the odds are at least **20 to 1** against their being random. Put another way, social scientists reject all findings when the probability they are random is greater than .05, or 5 in 100. What this level of significance means is that if 100 random samples were drawn independently from the same population, a difference this large would not turn up more than 5 times, purely by chance. In fact, many social scientists think this is too lenient a standard, and some even require that the probability that a finding is random be less than .01, or 1 in 100. To apply these rules of thumb, social scientists calculate the **level of significance** of the differences in question and compare them against these standards.

Let's see what the level of significance is for this table. *Press S (for Statistics).* Across the screen, under the words **Nominal Statistics,** we see: Chi-Square: 5.664 DF: 1 (Prob. = 0.017).

Chi-Square (often written as χ^2) is the name of the particular test of significance we are using. For now, you can ignore everything else on the screen except (Prob. = 0.017), which translates as the probability that this is a random result. Put another way, what this means is that if there is no difference between single and married individuals in the population as a whole, we would expect an observed difference this large by sheer chance only 17 times out of every 1,000 random samples. So the odds are extremely high that single and married people *do differ* in their fear of crime. In any event, the level of significance far exceeds the minimal .05 level. That is, we shall accept any finding when the probability of it being a random result is *smaller* than .05. If the test of significance had yielded a result of 0.051 or greater, then we would have rejected the hypothesis and assumed that single and married people do not differ in their fear of walking in their neighborhoods at night.

Press <ENTER> twice and you will be ready to run a new table. Our new hypothesis is: **People who have been burglarized in the past year will be more apt to be afraid to walk in their neighborhoods at night.**

This time let's use the F3 window to select the variables. *Press the F3 Key.* With the highlight on variable **1** or **FEAR WALK**, *press the left arrow key* to select it as the row variable. Now use the down arrow to place the highlight on **2** or **BURGLED?** and *press the left arrow key* to select it as the column variable. Now *press <ENTER>.* The two indicated variables will take their place on the screen as the row and column variables. *Press <ENTER> again and then again and the table will appear. Press C for column percentages.*

Part II - *ANALYZING CRIME DATA*

Exercise 4

	YES	NO
YES	57.4	41.7
NO	42.6	58.3

We see (by reading across and comparing) that people who were burglarized in the past year are more likely (57.4 percent) than those who were not burglarized (41.7) to say they are afraid to walk at night.

Press S (for Statistics). For this table Prob. = 0.000. That is far better than our standard of 0.050 — it means that a result like this would occur by chance less often than once in a thousand samples. Our hypothesis is supported.

Press <ENTER> twice and you will be ready to run a new table. The hypothesis is: **People who live in large cities will be more apt than those who live in suburbs, towns and rural areas to be afraid to walk around in their neighborhood at night.**

Make **1** or **FEAR WALK** the row variable and select **19** or **PLACE SIZE** as the column variable. The table appears on the screen. *Press C for column percentages.*

	CITY	SUBURB	TOWN	RURAL
YES	58.2	39.3	35.9	31.7
NO	41.8	60.7	64.1	68.3

Notice the flashing arrow at the top right of the screen. It is telling you that not all of the table can show on the screen at one time. Use the right arrow key to move the missing group onto the screen. The left arrow key will move them off again.

If you study the table for a moment you'll see our hypothesis seems to be supported. To make sure *press S (for Statistics)*. Here the probability is far smaller than our standard of 0.05 — it is 0.000. That means the odds of getting a finding this large through random errors are less than 1 chance in 1,000 samples.

Press <ENTER> twice and you will be ready to run a new table. The hypothesis is: **Women will be more apt than men to be afraid to walk around in their neighborhood at night.**

Make **1** or **FEAR WALK** the row variable and select **21** or **SEX** as the column variable. *Press <ENTER> twice.* The table appears on the screen. *Press C for column percentages.*

	MALE	FEMALE
YES	23.2	57.6
NO	76.8	42.4

Press S (for Statistics). Here too the probability is far smaller than our standard of 0.05 — it is 0.000. That means the odds of getting a finding this large through random errors are less than 1 chance in 1,000 samples. So, once again our hypothesis is strongly supported. The majority of women fear walking in their neighborhoods at night, while the majority of men do not.

Press <ENTER> twice and you will be ready to run a new table. The hypothesis is: **Higher-income people will be less afraid to walk in their neighborhoods than lower-income people will be.**

Make **1** or **FEAR WALK** the row variable and select **26** or **FAMILY $** as the column variable. *Press <ENTER> twice.* The table appears on the screen. *Press C for column percentages.*

	UNDER $12K	$12-$23K	$23-$35K	$35-$60K	OVER $60K
YES	53.4	54.6	40.7	34.1	39.9
NO	46.6	54.4	59.3	65.9	60.1

To see the last column on the right, *press the right arrow key.* From just looking at the percentages it is obvious that our hypothesis is supported. A majority of those with annual family incomes of less than $12,000 fear walking around in their neighborhoods at night, whereas most people with higher incomes are not fearful. *Press S (for Statistics).* We see that the probability is far smaller than our standard of 0.05 — it is 0.000. That means the odds of getting a finding this large through random errors are less than 1 time out of 1,000 samples.

Press <ENTER> twice and you will be ready to run a new table. This time we are going to reverse our hypothesis to see if fear of crime causes people to own guns: **People who are afraid to walk in their neighborhoods at night will be more apt to have purchased a gun.**

Make **15** or **OWN GUN?** the row variable and select **1** or **FEAR WALK** as the column variable. *Press <ENTER> twice.* The table appears on the screen. *Press C for column percentages.*

Exercise 4

	YES	NO
OWNS GUN	33.1	48.5
NO GUN	66.9	51.5

Not only is our hypothesis rejected, but the opposite relationship holds: People who are afraid are less likely to have a gun. *Press S (for Statistics)*. In fact, the probability is far smaller than our standard of 0.05 — it is 0.000.

Press <ENTER> twice and you will be ready to run a new table. The hypothesis is: **Fear of crime will be lower in the heartland: the Midwest and the Mountain regions.**

Make **1** or **FEAR WALK** the row variable and **18** or **REGION** the column variable. *Press C for column percentages*.

	EAST	MIDWEST	SOUTH	MOUNTAIN	PACIFIC
YES	41.2	38.0	44.9	28.3	54.1
NO	58.8	62.0	55.1	71.7	45.9

Our hypothesis seems to be supported. The Mountain and Midwest regions are noticeably lower than the rest of the nation. *Press S (for Statistics)*. And the differences are significant. Prob. = 0.000.

Now let's see if we can better understand *why* these regional differences exist.

The hypothesis is: **People will be more afraid of walking around their neighborhoods at night in places where homicide rates are high.**

Open the **FIFTYC** data file and go to the mapping function. Map **8** or **HOMICIDE**.

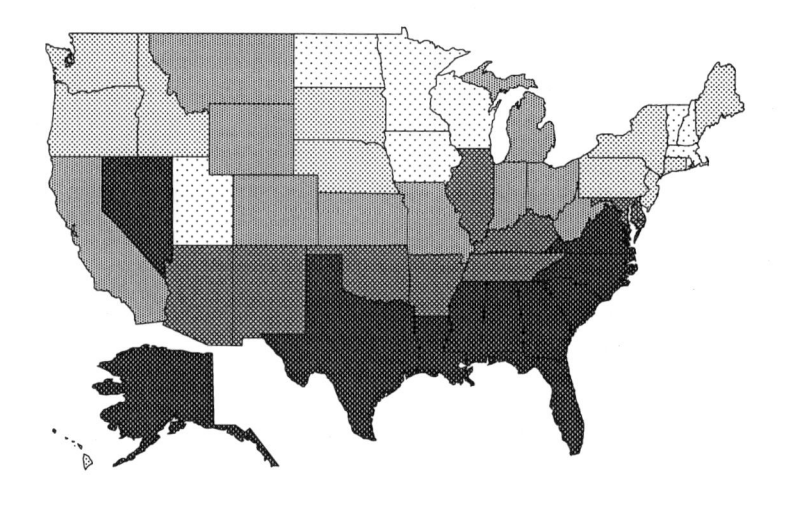

1992: Homicides per 100,000

44. CRIMINOLOGY - *An Introduction Using MicroCase*

Notice that the southern area plus New York and California are highest on homicides. *Press D (for Distribution)* to see all 50 states ranked from highest to lowest. Louisiana is highest followed by New York, Texas, California, Mississippi, Maryland, Illinois and Alabama. People are fearful about walking around at night where there are reasons to be fearful.

Now, it's your turn.

> **REVIEW**
>
> * A result is statistically significant when the probability that it is a random result is less than 1 in 20, or whenever Prob. = 0.050 *or less*. Thus, Prob. = 0.051 is not significant, while Prob. = 0.049 is.

Name: **Worksheets** - Exercise 4

> *Workbook exercises and software are copyrighted. Copying is prohibited by law.*

Open the **NORC** data file and select the Tabular Statistics function.

1. The hypothesis is: **African-Americans will be more likely than whites to fear walking in their neighborhoods at night.**

   Make **1** or **FEAR WALK** the row variable and **23** or **WH/AF-A** the column variable. *Press C for column percentages.* Fill in the table.

	WHITE	AFRICAN-AM
YES	%	%
NO	%	%

   Prob. = _____

   Is the difference statistically significant? (circle one)   YES   NO

   Is the hypothesis supported or rejected? (circle one)   SUPPORTED   REJECTED

   Can you suggest reasons for this particular outcome?

Part II - *ANALYZING CRIME DATA*

Worksheets - Exercise 4

2. The hypothesis is: **Older people will be more likely than younger people to fear walking in their neighborhoods at night**.

    Make **1** or **FEAR WALK** the row variable and **25** or **AGE** the column variable. *Press C for column percentages.* Fill in the table.

	18-29	30-39	40-49	50-65	OVER 65
YES	%	%	%	%	%
NO	%	%	%	%	%

    Prob. = _____

    Is the difference statistically significant? (circle one) YES NO

    Is the hypothesis supported or rejected? (circle one) SUPPORTED REJECTED

    Can you suggest reasons for this particular outcome?

Name: *Worksheets* - Exercise 4

3. The hypothesis is: **People who fear walking in their neighborhoods at night will be more likely than those who aren't fearful to favor a gun control law.**

   Make **14** or **GUN LAW?** the row variable and **1** or **FEAR WALK** the column variable. *Press C for column percentages.* Fill in the table.

	YES	NO
FAVOR	%	%
OPPOSE	%	%

   Prob. = _____

   Is the difference statistically significant? **(circle one)**   YES   NO

   Is the hypothesis supported or rejected? **(circle one)**   SUPPORTED   REJECTED

   Can you suggest reasons for this particular outcome?

Part II - *ANALYZING CRIME DATA*

Worksheets - Exercise 4

4. The hypothesis is: **People who fear walking in their neighborhoods at night will be more likely than those who aren't fearful to think the government should spend more on crime prevention.**

   Make **8** or **CRIME $** the row variable and **1** or **FEAR WALK** the column variable. *Press C for column percentages.* Fill in the table.

	YES	NO
TOO LITTLE	%	%
RIGHT	%	%
TOO MUCH	%	%

   Prob. = _____

   Is the difference statistically significant? (circle one)   YES   NO

   Is the hypothesis supported or rejected? (circle one)   SUPPORTED   REJECTED

   Can you suggest reasons for this particular outcome?

EXERCISE 5: Auto Theft: Scatterplots and Correlation

Open the **FIFTYC** data file and go to the red **STATISTICAL ANALYSIS MENU**. *Place* the highlight on **E. Mapping Variables** and *press* <ENTER>. Now the screen asks you for the name or number of the variable you wish to map. *Type* **14** or **AUTO THEFT** and *press* <ENTER>. What you are mapping is the official (UCR) rate of reported auto thefts. Technically speaking, this is the motor vehicle theft rate, since all stolen motor-driven vehicles (including motorcycles) are included in it. But, because more than 80 percent of the incidents involve an automobile, we will conform to the common practice of calling it the auto theft or car theft rate.

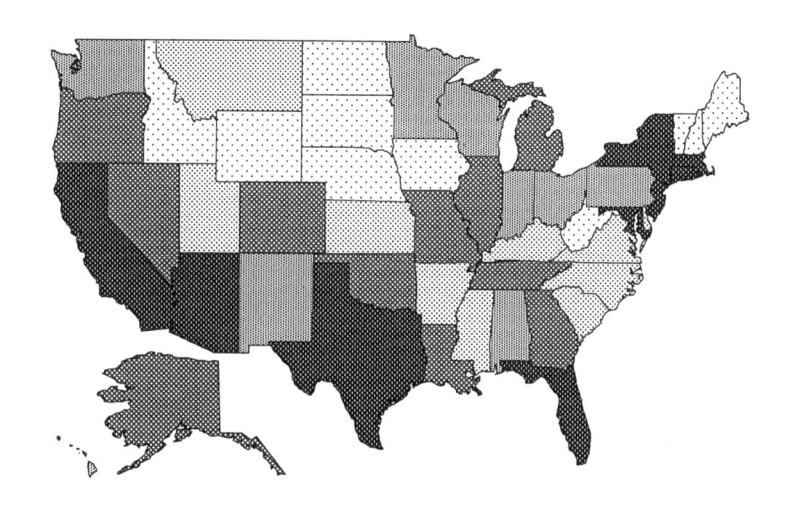

1992: Vehicle thefts per 100,000

Type N (for Name) to see which state has the highest official auto theft rate.

California is highest with 1037 stolen cars per 100,000 population. *Press the down arrow* to see the next highest state. New York is just behind California with 932. Florida is third and Texas fourth. *Now press D (for Distribution)* to see all 50 states ranked from high to low. South Dakota, Vermont and Maine are lowest.

Next look at another map: **26** or **% METROPOL**. This map shows the percent of the population in each state who live in metropolitan areas — large cities and their nearby suburbs.

Exercise 5

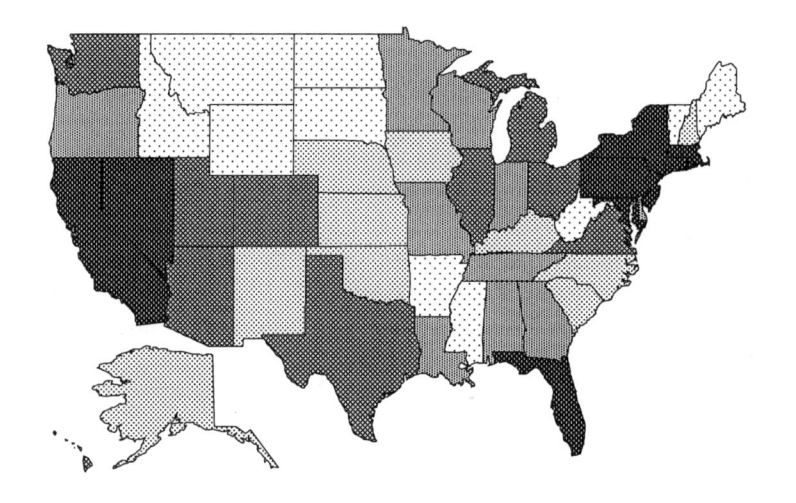

1988: Percent of the population living in Metropolitan Statistical Areas

Type N (for Name) to see which state is the most metropolitan state. New Jersey is — everyone there lives in a large city or the suburb of one. California is second with 95.7 of its population in metropolitan areas. *Now press D (for Distribution)* to see all 50 states ranked from high to low. Notice that New York is only in sixth place and that Idaho is the least metropolitan state, followed by Vermont.

Also notice how very much alike these two maps are. Both reveal a bi-coastal pattern. The auto theft rate and the percent metropolitan are both highest in the states along the Pacific and the Atlantic states of the Northeast.

When you did Exercise 1 you no doubt found it easy to notice when two maps are this much alike. But, as you examined maps that were less alike you must have found it more difficult to say how much alike they were.

It also becomes more difficult to say how alike any two maps are when the maps are very complex. For example, it would be much harder to compare two maps based on the 3,142 counties of the United States than two maps based on the 50 states. The same is true of attempts to compare lists. It is not too hard to compare the distributions of the auto theft rates and the percent metropolitan and to notice that the same states tended to be high or low both times. But it would have been much harder with a longer list. Thus it was a considerable achievement when, in the 1890s, an Englishman named Karl Pearson discovered an incredibly simple method for comparing maps or lists.

To see Pearson's method we can draw a horizontal line across the bottom of a piece of paper. We will let this line represent the map of percent metropolitan. So, at the left end of this line we will write 20.0, which indicates the state with the lowest rate: Idaho. At the right end of the line we will place the number 100.0 to represent New Jersey as the state with the highest rate.

20.0   100.0

Now we can draw a vertical line up the left side of the paper. This line will represent the map of the auto theft rate. At the bottom of this line we will write 101 to represent South Dakota, the lowest state. At the top we will write 1037 to represent California, the highest state.

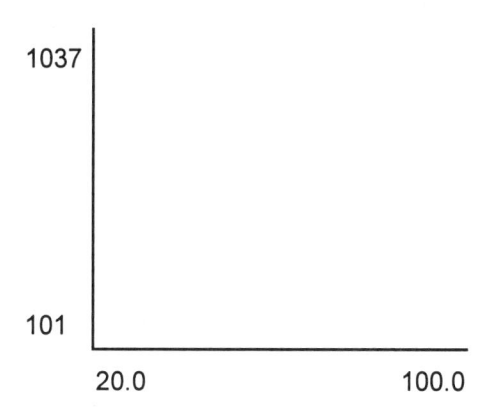

```
1037 |
     |
     |
     |
     |
     |
 101 |_____
        20.0        100.0
```

Now that we have a line with an appropriate scale to represent each map, the next thing we need to do is refer to the distributions for each map in order to learn the value of each state and then locate it on each line according to its score. Let's start with New Jersey. Since it is the most metropolitan we can easily find its place on the horizontal line above. Make a small mark at 100.0 to locate New Jersey. Next, New Jersey was sixth highest in terms of its auto theft rate, so estimate where its rate of 816 is located on the vertical line. Knowing where New Jersey is on each line representing each map, we can draw a vertical line up from its position on percent metropolitan and we can draw a horizontal line out from its position on auto theft. Where these two lines meet (or cross) we can make a dot. This dot represents the combined map location for New Jersey.

Next, let's locate California. Its percent metropolitan is 95.7, so we can make a mark on the horizontal line at that spot. Its auto theft rate was highest at 1037, so we can mark that point on the vertical line. Now we draw a line up from the mark on the horizontal line and draw one out from the mark on the vertical line. Where these two lines intersect we can make another dot, which represents the combined map location for California.

When we have followed this procedure for each state, we will have 50 dots located within the space defined by the vertical and horizontal lines representing the two maps. What we have done is to create a **scatterplot**. Fortunately, you don't have to go to all this trouble. *MicroCase* will do it for you. Return to the red **STATISTICAL ANALYSIS MENU** and select **F. Scatterplot**. Make **14** or **AUTO THEFT** the dependent variable and *press <ENTER>*. Now make **26** or **% METROPOL** the independent variable and *press <ENTER>*. Press <ENTER> again. This screen will appear:

Exercise 5

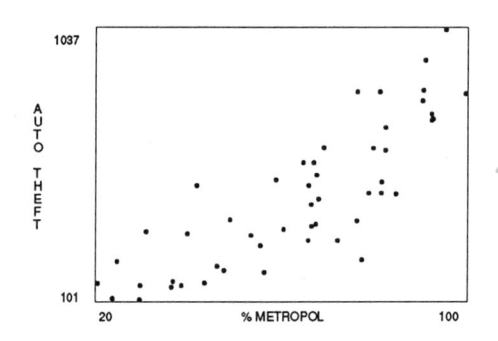

```
1037
A
U
T
O
T
H
E
F
T
101
    20        % METROPOL        100
```

Current: r = 0.828   Prob. = 0.000   N = 50   Miss. = 0

reg. Line   Resid.   Outliers   Show case   X label   Y label   Print

Each of these dots is a state. *Press S (for Show case) and then type* **UTAH**. See the dot that is flashing on the screen? That dot represents Utah's combined position on the two maps. *Press <ENTER> to cause the dot to stop flashing. Press <ENTER> again* to exit the Show case option. You can examine the dot for each state in this way. If you have forgotten precisely what either of the two maps represents, you can examine their long labels by *pressing X for the horizontal map and y for the vertical map.*

Once Pearson had created a scatterplot, his next step was to calculate what he called the regression line. To see this line simply *press L (for Line)*. This line represents the best effort to draw a straight line that connects all of the dots. It is unnecessary for you to know how to calculate the location of the regression line — the program does it for you. But, if you would like to see how the regression line would look if all of the dots were along a straight line, all you need to do is examine the scatterplot for identical maps. So, if you create a scatterplot using **14** or **AUTO THEFT** as both the dependent and independent variables, you will be comparing identical maps and the dots representing states will all be on the regression line like a string of beads.

However, since the maps for auto theft and for the percent metropolitan are only very similar, but not identical, most of the dots are scattered near, but not on, the regression line. Pearson's method for calculating how much alike are any two maps or lists is very easy, once the regression line has been drawn. What it amounts to is measuring the distance out from the regression line to every dot. To do this, simply *press R (for Residual)*. See all the little lines. If you added them together, you would have a sum of the deviation of the dots from the regression line. The smaller this sum, the more alike are the two maps. For example, when the maps are identical and all the dots are on the regression line, the sum of the deviations is 0.

In order to make it simple to interpret results, Pearson invented a procedure to convert the sums into a number he called the **correlation coefficient**. The correlation coefficient varies from 0.0 to 1.0. When maps are identical, the correlation coefficient will be 1.0. When they are completely unalike, the correlation coefficient will be 0.0. Correlations may be either positive or negative. When two maps are perfect opposites the correlation coefficient will be −1.0. Thus, the closer the correlation coefficient is to 1.0 the more alike the two maps or lists. Pearson used the letter **r** as the symbol for his correlation coefficient. Look at the lower left-hand corner of the screen and you will see **r = 0.828**. This indicates that the maps are very similar. To the right of the correlation coefficient you will find **statistical significance** — the odds that this is a chance finding. Prob. = 0.000 indicates that the correlation is highly significant.

The point of calculating correlations is to discover links between various social phenomena. For example, we already have seen that there are huge differences in auto theft from one state to another. Now suppose we ask "why?" What could be causing these differences? Suppose we decided that a lack of police protection might hold at least part of the answer. That is, we are claiming that states with proportionately more law enforcement officers will have lower rates of auto theft. This claim cannot be true unless there is a substantial negative correlation between **14** or **AUTO THEFT** and **23** or **COPS/10000**.

To see if this is the case, all we need to do is create a scatterplot of these two variables. When we do we will find that the correlation coefficient is 0.631. However, this is a positive, not a negative, correlation. We can tell that in two ways. First, there is no negative sign in front of the correlation coefficient. Second, the regression line slopes upward from left to right, showing that as the number of police per 10,000 *rises*, so does the auto theft rate. That completely refutes our claim that a lack of police protection causes higher auto theft rates.

Keep in mind, however, that correlation and causation are *not* the same thing. It is true that without correlation there can be no causation. Thus a lack of police protection can not be considered as a possible cause of auto theft *if* there is no correlation between the two. But, correlations often occur between two variables without one being a cause of the other. For example, in any grade school you would find a very high correlation between children's height and their reading ability. This correlation occurs because both height and reading ability reflect age — the taller kids are older and the older kids read better. The positive correlation between the number of police per 10,000 and the auto theft rate may be another example of a non-causal correlation. Surely no one would suggest that by hiring more police, city governments *cause* their auto theft rates to rise. More likely, this correlation does reflect a cause-and-effect relationship, but in the *reverse* direction: Rising auto theft rates *cause* governments to hire more police. But, it also could be that auto thefts don't cause police hiring, but that high rates of both are simply facets of a common, underlying cause — that both are parts of contemporary urban life. That is, both police and auto thieves abound in major metropolitan areas.

As mentioned above, correlation coefficients can be either positive or negative. In the first two scatterplots we discovered positive correlations — where auto theft is higher, the proportion of metropolitan residents and the number of police per 10,000 are higher too. That is, as one rises so does the other — they tend to occur in unison. But, when we examine a new scatterplot the whole picture changes radically. Use **14** or **AUTO THEFT** as the dependent variable and **58** or **FLD&STREAM** as the independent variable.

When you examine this scatterplot you will see that where the circulation rate for *Field & Stream Magazine* is higher, the auto theft rate is lower: Out in the wide open spaces where a lot of people hunt and fish and read magazines devoted to those activities, there is less auto theft. *Press L (for Line)*.

Exercise 5

Notice that in this case the regression line slopes downward from left to right, rather than upward. That always indicates a negative correlation. And notice that a minus sign now precedes the correlation coefficient: −.758.

Finally, let's see a scatterplot of two variables that are not correlated. Use **64** or **PEACE CORP** as the dependent variable and **60** or **PICKUPS** as the independent variable. Did more people join the Peace Corps from states in which the rate of pickup truck ownership is high? No. The relationship between these two variables is essentially random. The dots are scattered all over the screen. *Press L (for Line)*. The regression line has no slope and simply crosses the screen from left to right. And the correlation coefficient is a minuscule -0.002.

We have seen that correlation does not necessarily demonstrate causation — variables may be highly correlated without one being the cause of the other. It would seem silly to suggest, for example, that the correlation between *Field & Stream* circulation and auto theft reflects cause-and-effect. Nevertheless, social scientists examine correlations primarily to test hypotheses that propose cause-and-effect relationships.

To more fully capture this aspect of research, it will be helpful to distinguish between **independent** and **dependent variables**. If we think something might be the cause of something else, we say that *the cause is the independent variable* and that the *consequence (or the thing that is being caused) is the dependent variable*. To help you remember the difference, think that variables being caused are dependent on the causal variable, whereas causal variables are not dependent, but are independent. That's why the scatterplot screen gives you the option to identify one variable as dependent and the other as independent.

While the scatterplot was a brilliant invention, and is still essential for analyzing aggregate data, the correlation coefficient can be computed directly. To explore this, shift to **G. Correlation**. When the screen asks for the name or number of variable 1: *type* **14** or **AUTO THEFT** and *press <ENTER>*. Use **50** or **ABORTION** as the second variable, **71** or **%BEER** as the third, and **65** or **COKE USERS** as the fourth and then *press <ENTER> twice*. This screen will appear:

	AUTO THEFT	ABORTION	%BEER	COKE USERS
AUTO THEFT	1.000	0.664**	-0.467**	0.579**
ABORTION	0.664**	1.000	-0.731**	0.506**
%BEER	-0.467**	-0.731**	1.000	-0.265*
COKE USER	0.579**	0.506**	-0.265*	1.000

You can discover the correlation between any two variables in either of two ways. First, find one of the two variables in the horizontal list across the top of the screen. Then look down that column until you come to the second variable as shown in the vertical list to the left of the screen. Thus you will see that the correlation between the abortion rate and the auto theft rate is 0.664. You can do it the other way too, looking for one variable at the left and then looking for the other across the top. When a variable is correlated with itself

56.   CRIMINOLOGY - *An Introduction Using MicroCase*

the result is always perfect — 1.000. All correlations that meet the 0.050 level of statistical significance are indicated by one asterisk, and two asterisks indicate significance above the 0.010 level. All of these are highly significant, although all of the correlations involving beer drinking are negative. And most support the notion that what we are looking at are not causal relations, but various aspects of urban lifestyles. That is, it seems unlikely that drinking beer prevents people from stealing cars any more than auto theft causes abortions. It seems entirely possible, however, that there is a causal relationship between the rate of cocaine addiction and auto theft — as we shall explore in Exercise 7.

Your turn.

Name: Worksheets - Exercise 5

Workbook exercises and software are copyrighted. Copying is prohibited by law.

1. *Open* the **FIFTYC** data file and select the scatterplot function. Create the following scatterplot:

    Dependent variable: **14** or **AUTO THEFT**
    Independent variable: **70** or **% WINE**

    Write down the long label for **70** or **% WINE**: (Press X to see it) _____

    _____
    _____

    What is the correlation coefficient?   r = _____

    Is this a positive or negative correlation?   (circle one)   POS   NEG

    Is the difference statistically significant?   (circle one)   YES   NO

    Might this be a cause-and-effect relationship? Suggest why or why not.

2. Create the following scatterplot:

    Dependent variable: **14** or **AUTO THEFT**
    Independent variable: **57** or **TV DISHES**

    Write in the long label for **57** or **TV DISHES**: (Press X to see it) _____

    _____
    _____

Part II - *ANALYZING CRIME DATA*

Worksheets - Exercise 5

What is the correlation coefficient? r = _____

Is this a positive or negative correlation? (circle one) POS   NEG

Might this be a cause-and-effect relationship? Suggest why or why not.

3. Create the following scatterplot:

    Dependent variable: **14** or **AUTO THEFT**
    Independent variable: **60** or **PICKUPS**

    Write in the long label for **60** *or* **PICKUPS**: (Press X to see it) _____

    _____

    _____

    What is the correlation coefficient? r = _____

    Is this a positive or negative correlation? (circle one) POS   NEG

    Might this be a cause-and-effect relationship? Suggest why or why not.

Name: **Worksheets** - Exercise 5

4. Create the following scatterplot:

   Dependent variable: **14** or **AUTO THEFT**
   Independent variable: **110** or **SYPHILIS**

   *Write down the long label for **110** or **SYPHILIS**:* (Press X to see it) _____

   _____

   _____

   What is the correlation coefficient? r = _____

   Is this a positive or negative correlation? (circle one)   POS   NEG

   Might this be a cause-and-effect relationship? Suggest why or why not.

5. Create the following scatterplot:

   Dependent variable: **14** or **AUTO THEFT**
   Independent variable: **49** or **% DROPOUTS**

   *Write down the long label for **49** or **% DROPOUTS**:* (Press X to see it) _____

   _____

   _____

   What is the correlation coefficient? r = _____

   Is this a positive or negative correlation? (circle one)   POS   NEG

Part II - ANALYZING CRIME DATA

Worksheets - Exercise 5

Might this be a cause-and-effect relationship? Suggest why or why not.

6. Create the following scatterplot:

   Dependent variable: **14** or **AUTO THEFT**
   Independent variable: **30** or **$PER CAPIT**

   Write down the long label for **30** *or* **$PER CAPIT**: (Press X to see it) _____

   _____

   _____

   What is the correlation coefficient? r = _____

   Is this a positive or negative correlation? (circle one) POS NEG

   Might this be a cause-and-effect relationship? Suggest why or why not.

62. CRIMINOLOGY - *An Introduction Using MicroCase*

Name: _____ **Worksheets** - Exercise 5

7. Clear the scatterplot screen and then use the F3 window and the right arrow key to see the long labels for each of the items below. Write them down.

48 or **% COLLEGE** _____

_____

_____

59 or **COSMO** _____

_____

_____

106 or **% FEM.WORK** _____

_____

_____

43 or **% FEMHEAD** _____

_____

_____

Go to the *Correlation* function and use **14** or **AUTO THEFT** plus all four of these variables. Fill in the following correlation matrix:

	AUTO THEFT	% COLLEGE	COSMO	% FEM.WORK	% FEMHEAD
AUTO THEFT					
% COLLEGE					
COSMO					
% FEM.WORK					
% FEMHEAD					

What is the correlation between auto theft and percent of women in the labor force? _____

Is it significant? **(circle one)**   YES .01   YES .05   NO

Part II - ANALYZING CRIME DATA

Worksheets - Exercise 5

What is the correlation between Cosmopolitan Magazine circulation and percent of women in the labor force? _____

Is it significant? (circle one) YES .01   YES .05   NO

Could this reflect a cause-and-effect relationship? Explain.

What is the correlation between auto theft and Cosmopolitan Magazine circulation? _____

Is it significant? (circle one) YES .01   YES .05   NO

Could this reflect a cause-and-effect relationship? Explain.

PART III: *DRUGS AND ALCOHOL*

In 1990, 1.4 million Americans were arrested for drunk driving, 716,504 were arrested for drunkenness, and 552,039 for violations of liquor laws. Another 869,155 were arrested for drug abuse violations. In addition, many of those arrested for more serious crimes such as murder, assault, rape, and robbery were under the influence of alcohol or drugs when they committed the offense.

Are these large numbers? That depends on how they are interpreted. On the one hand, 122 million Americans say that they drink alcoholic beverages. If no one was arrested twice for a liquor violation in 1990, then 2 percent of those who drink got in trouble with the police for liquor violations. But, we know that repeat offenders are very common in these arrest categories, so the total number of drinkers who got arrested probably was no more than 1 percent. On the other hand, most people who sometimes drive while under the influence of alcohol don't get caught and no one is arrested for drunkenness unless they go out in public while drunk. People who frequently get drunk, but only at home, do not get arrested. As for drugs, obviously only a small fraction of those who use them get arrested for it. In any event, however one assesses these numbers they would seem sufficiently large to justify the conclusion that there is an alcohol and drug "problem" in our society.

The following four exercises explore aspects of alcohol and drug use. Later exercises will examine links between drugs and alcohol and other categories of offenses.

EXERCISE 6: Getting Drunk in America

You are about to test this hypothesis: **Men are more apt than women to go to bars and taverns.**

Open the **NORC** data file and select **B. Tabular Statistics** from the **STATISTICAL ANALYSIS MENU**. Now the screen asks you for the name or number of the row variable. *Type* **11** or **GO TO BARS** and *press <ENTER>*. Make **21** or **SEX** the column variable. When the screen asks for a control variable, simply *press <ENTER>*. When the screen asks for a subset variable, simply *press <ENTER>*. When this table appears on the screen *press C for column percentages*.

	MALE	FEMALE
WEEKLY	13.3	5.0
SOMETIMES	45.5	34.5
NEVER	41.2	60.5

The hypothesis is supported: Men are more than twice as likely as women to go to bars once a week or oftener. *Press S (for Statistics)*. The probability of these being random differences is minuscule — Prob. = 0.000.

Part III - *DRUGS AND ALCOHOL*

Exercise 6

Press <ENTER> twice and you will be ready to run a new table. The hypothesis is: **Men are more likely than women to drink alcoholic beverages.**

Make **12** or **DRINK?** the row variable, and select **21** or **SEX** as the column variable. When the table appears on the screen *press C for column percentages.*

	MALE	FEMALE
USE ALC	75.0	65.7
ABSTAINS	25.0	34.3

The hypothesis is supported. *Press S (for Statistics).* The probability of these being random differences is 0.000. Notice, however, that the gender differences in the percent who drink are not nearly so large as are differences in going to bars.

Press <ENTER> twice and you will be ready to run a new table. The hypothesis is: **Men are more likely than women to get drunk.**

Make **13** or **DRUNK** the row variable, and select **21** or **SEX** as the column variable. When the table appears on the screen *press C for column percentages.*

	MALE	FEMALE
GETS DRUNK	30.8	16.2
NO	44.1	49.2
ABSTAINS	25.1	34.6

The hypothesis is supported: Men are far more likely to get drunk. *Press S (for Statistics).* The probability of these being random differences is 0.000.

Now, instead of asking who gets drunk, let's see if it matters *where people do their drinking.*

Press <ENTER> twice and you will be ready to run a new table. The hypothesis is: **People who drink in bars and taverns are more likely to get drunk.**

Make **13** or **DRUNK** the row variable, and select **11** or **GO TO BARS** as the column variable. When the table appears on the screen *press C for column percentages.*

	WEEKLY	SOMETIMES	NEVER
GETS DRUNK	57.9	36.8	7.6
NO	37.2	56.8	40.7
ABSTAINS	5.0	6.3	51.7

The hypothesis is strongly supported. More than half of those who go to a bar or a tavern at least once a week or more often say they sometimes drink too much. Fewer than 8 percent of those who never go to a bar or tavern say they sometimes drink too much. *Press S (for Statistics)*. The probability of these being random differences is less than 0.000.

Now, you should notice something else about the information on the statistics screen. In addition to showing the probability that a difference this great arose by chance, the screen shows V = 0.398. V stands for Cramer's V and is used for cross-tabulations like this. V is calculated much like r, the correlation coefficient invented by Pearson which we examined in Exercise 5. For a variety of reasons that need not concern you until you take a statistics course, correlations on aggregate data tend to be much higher than those based on survey data. Thus, a V of this size is regarded as very strong. In any event, you will have significance to depend on in deciding whether a hypothesis is supported or rejected by the data.

At this point an analyst might wonder whether going to bars has the same impact on men as on women, in terms of drinking too much. To find out, we are going to use sex as **a control variable**. When you make something a control variable, you are asking that separate tables be created for each category of that variable. In this instance, you will examine two tables showing the relationship between getting drunk and going to bars and taverns, one for males and one for females.

Make **13** or **DRUNK** the row variable, and select **11** or **GO TO BARS** as the column variable. However, this time when the screen asks for a control variable *type 21 or SEX and then press <ENTER>. Press <ENTER> twice.* When the table appears on the screen *press C for column percentages*.

MALE

	WEEKLY	SOMETIMES	NEVER
GETS DRUNK	57.0	44.2	13.4
NO	36.7	49.6	39.0
ABSTAINS	6.3	6.1	47.7

This table includes **only** men. How can you tell? Look at the upper left corner of the screen. There the word **CONTROLS** appears. Beneath is **SEX:MALE**. That means sex is the control variable and that this table is limited to men. Notice that the table is very similar to the one above which included both men and women. *Press S (for Statistics)*. Here too the relationship is highly significant (Prob. = 0.000). However, V is slightly lower (V = 0.369).

Press <ENTER> to return to the table for males, and then *press <ENTER>* again. Now the table based on females is on the screen. *Press C for column percentages*.

Part III - DRUGS AND ALCOHOL

Exercise 6

FEMALE

	WEEKLY	SOMETIMES	NEVER
GETS DRUNK	59.5	30.4	4.4
NO	38.1	63.0	41.6
ABSTAINS	2.4	6.5	53.9

It also is nearly identical with the original table. *Press S (for Statistics)*. Again, the relationship is highly significant (Prob. = 0.000) and V is a bit higher (V = 0.409).

We must conclude that going to bars influences men and women to about the same extent.

A substantial part of this effect may be that people who don't drink, seldom go to bars or taverns — maybe we should limit our analysis to people who drink. To do this we will use the **subset** function for the first time. Using a control variable causes separate tables to be created for each category of the variable. The subset function allows you to limit the table to certain features of the variable used for subsetting.

Make **13** or **DRUNK** the row variable, and select **11** or **GO TO BARS** as the column variable. When the screen asks for a control variable *press <ENTER>*. However, when the screen asks for the name or number of variable 1 for defining subset, *type* **12** or **DRINK?** and then *press <ENTER>*. The screen asks for the **lower limit**. Since we wish to limit the data to those who drink, and since they constitute category 1, *type* **1** and *press <ENTER>*. Now the screen asks for the upper limit. Again *type* **1** and *press <ENTER>*. When the screen asks for variable 2 for defining subset simply *press <ENTER>*. *Press C for column percentages*.

	WEEKLY	SOMETIMES	NEVER
GETS DRUNK	60.9	39.3	15.8
NO	39.1	60.7	84.2

What you have done is limited the table to persons in category 1 on variable 12. You can tell this because at the upper left of the screen is the name of the subset variable: DRINK? Next to it, across the top of the screen, is the line SUBSET WITH VALUE USE ALC, which is the name of the category you selected for a subset. Another way to tell is that there are no cases of persons who abstain — they all were omitted by the subset.

With non-drinkers omitted, the proportion who get drunk is higher in each category of variable 11 — even among those who never go to bars or taverns, 15.8 percent report drinking too much. The impact of going to bars on getting drunk remains strong, but seems a bit less strong than when the abstainers were included. *Press S (for Statistics)*. Again, the relationship is highly significant (Prob. = 0.000). However, V is moderately reduced (V = 0.309), confirming that the effect is a bit weaker.

Not everyone is equally likely to go to bars. The hypothesis is: **Single and divorced people are much more likely than married people to go to bars.**

Make **11** or **GO TO BARS** the row variable, and select **35** or **MARITAL** as the column variable. When the table appears on the screen *press C for column percentages*.

	MARRIED	WIDOWED	DIVORCED	NEV.MARRY
WEEKLY	4.7	4.1	12.7	18.7
SOMETIMES	39.4	11.2	48.0	47.9
NEVER	55.9	84.7	39.3	33.4

The hypothesis is strongly supported. Never-married persons were more than four times as likely to say they go to bars weekly as were married people. The majority of married people reported never going to bars as compared with only about a third of divorced and never-married people. *Press S (for Statistics)*. Prob. = 0.000. V = 0.234.

Bars are not only places to drink. Many of them serve as the scene for seeking sexual partners — bars are places where one can meet people, many of whom are not entirely sober.

Press <ENTER> twice and you will be ready to run a new table. The hypothesis is: **The more sex partners that people have had in the past year, the more likely they are to go to bars.**

Make **11** or **GO TO BARS** the row variable, and select **20** or **SEX PARTNR** as the column variable. When the table appears on the screen *press C for column percentages*.

	NONE	ONE	2 OR MORE
WEEKLY	3.5	7.0	28.6
SOMETIMES	20.8	45.1	53.2
NEVER	75.8	47.8	18.3

The hypothesis is strongly supported. Three-fourths of those who did not have a sexual partner during the past year never went to a bar, whereas more than 80 percent of those with 2 or more partners during the year went to a bar at least sometimes. *Press S (for Statistics)*. Prob. = 0.000. V = 0.265.

Now let's examine this relationship within each gender.

Make **11** or **GO TO BARS** the row variable, and select **20** or **SEX PARTNR** as the column variable. However, this time when the screen asks for a control variable *type* **21** or **SEX**. When the table appears on the screen *press C for column percentages*.

Exercise 6

MALES

	NONE	ONE	2 OR MORE
WEEKLY	9.4	9.5	30.1
SOMETIMES	30.9	50.4	52.3
NEVER	59.7	40.1	17.6

The relationship remains strong among males. Those with two or more sexual partners during the past year are more than three times as likely to go to bars as those who had no or only one sexual partner. Indeed, only 17.6 percent of those with two or more partners never went to bars. *Press S (for Statistics)*. Prob. = 0.000. V = 0.213.

Press <ENTER> twice to see the table for females. Press C for column percentages.

FEMALES

	NONE	ONE	2 OR MORE
WEEKLY	0.9	5.1	26.3
SOMETIMES	16.4	41.1	54.5
NEVER	82.7	53.8	19.2

The relationship is even stronger among females. Virtually no women (0.9%) who lacked a sexual partner during the previous year went to bars weekly and 82.7 percent never did. But, of those with two or more sexual partners during the past year, only 19.2 percent never went to bars. *Press S (for Statistics)*. Prob. = 0.000. V = 0.281.

This is not to say that going to bars *causes* people to acquire new sexual partners; it is equally likely that people often go to bars seeking new sexual partners. Causation is not really the issue. Rather, what we have uncovered is a set of behaviors that form a package: being single or divorced, drinking, going to bars, having sexual encounters.

We have seen that getting drunk is influenced by where people drink. Now let's see if where people live influences drinking behavior.

Press <ENTER> twice and you will be ready to run a new table. The hypothesis is: **People who live in big cities or suburbs are more likely than those who live in small towns and rural areas to get drunk.**

Make **13** or **DRUNK** the row variable, and select **19** or **PLACE SIZE** as the column variable. When the table appears on the screen *press C for column percentages*.

	CITY	SUBURB	TOWN	RURAL
GETS DRUNK	22.8	22.9	19.8	18.9
NO	51.6	49.1	44.6	36.5
ABSTAINS	25.6	27.9	35.5	44.7

The influence of place size is not primarily on getting drunk, as rural residents are about as likely to get drunk as are people in large cities. Rather, the effect is on drinking at all. Notice that residents of small towns and rural areas are substantially more likely to abstain. *Press S (for Statistics)*. The differences are highly significant (Prob. = 0.000) and V = 0.097.

To see this even more clearly, make **12** or **DRINK?** the row variable, and select **19** or **PLACE SIZE** as the column variable. When the table appears on the screen *press C for column percentages*. Examine the table for a moment and then *press S (for Statistics)*. The differences are highly significant (Prob. = 0.000) and V increases to 0.137.

Press <ENTER> twice and you will be ready to run a new table. The hypothesis is: **People who live in the East and the Pacific regions are more likely than those who live in other regions to drink.**

Make **12** or **DRINK?** the row variable, and select **18** or **REGION** as the column variable. When the table appears on the screen *press C for column percentages*.

	EAST	MIDWEST	SOUTH	MOUNTAIN	PACIFIC
DRINKS	80.3	72.7	59.4	55.9	79.1
ABSTAINS	19.7	27.3	40.6	44.1	20.9

The hypothesis is supported. *Press S (for Statistics)*. The probability of these being random differences is 0.000 and V = 0.199.

Now open the **FIFTYC** data file and go to the mapping function. Map variable **105** or **CIRRHOSIS**. This is the annual death rate from cirrhosis of the liver per 100,000 population. Cirrhosis is almost always the result of many years of acute alcoholism.

Notice that the highest states are in the East and the Far West. *Type D (for Distribution)*. Notice that Nevada has the highest rate, followed by New York, New Mexico, California, Florida, Delaware, New Jersey and Massachusetts. Utah is the lowest.

These results very closely match the findings from the national survey.

Your turn.

Name: **Worksheets** - Exercise 6

Workbook exercises and software are copyrighted. Copying is prohibited by law.

Open the **NORC** data file and select the Tabular Statistics function.

1. The hypothesis is: **African-Americans will be more likely than whites to get drunk.**

    Make **13** or **DRUNK** the row variable and **23** or **WH/AF-A** the column variable. *Press C for column percentages.* Fill in the table.

	WHITE	AFRICAN-AM
GETS DRUNK	%	%
NO	%	%
ABSTAINS	%	%

    V = _____ Prob. = _____

    Is the difference statistically significant? **(circle one)**   YES   NO

    Is the hypothesis supported or rejected? **(circle one)**   SUPPORTED   REJECTED

    Does this result surprise you? Explain.

Part III - *DRUGS AND ALCOHOL*   73.

Worksheets - Exercise 6

2. The hypothesis is: **Younger people will be more likely than older people to get drunk.**

   Make **13** or **DRUNK** the row variable and **25** or **AGE** the column variable. *Press C for column percentages.* Fill in the table.

	18-29	30-39	40-49	50-65	OVER 65
GETS DRUNK	%	%	%	%	%
NO	%	%	%	%	%
ABSTAINS	%	%	%	%	%

   V = _____ Prob. = _____

   Is the difference statistically significant? **(circle one)**   YES   NO

   Is the hypothesis supported or rejected? **(circle one)**   SUPPORTED   REJECTED

   Does this result surprise you? Explain.

Name: **_Worksheets_** - Exercise 6

3. The hypothesis is: **Lower-income people will be more likely than upper-income people to get drunk.**

    Make **13** or **DRUNK** the row variable and **26** or **FAMILY $** the column variable. *Press C for column percentages.* Fill in the table.

	UNDER $12K	$12K-$23K	$23-$35K	$35-$60K	OVER $60K
GETS DRUNK	%	%	%	%	%
NO	%	%	%	%	%
ABSTAINS	%	%	%	%	%

    V = _____   Prob. = _____

    Is the difference statistically significant? **(circle one)**   YES   NO

    Is the hypothesis supported or rejected? **(circle one)**   SUPPORTED   REJECTED

    Does this result surprise you? Explain.

Part III - *DRUGS AND ALCOHOL*   75.

Worksheets - Exercise 6

4. The hypothesis is: **Gun owners will be more likely to get drunk than those who don't own guns**.

   Make **13** or **DRUNK** the row variable and **15** or **OWN GUN?** the column variable. *Press C for column percentages.* Fill in the table.

	YES	NO GUN
GETS DRUNK	%	%
NO	%	%
ABSTAINS	%	%

   V = _____ Prob. = _____

   Is the difference statistically significant? (circle one)   YES   NO

   Is the hypothesis supported or rejected? (circle one)   SUPPORTED   REJECTED

   Does this result surprise you? Explain.

Name: **Worksheets** - Exercise 6

5. The hypothesis is: **People who attend church frequently will be less likely than people who seldom attend church to get drunk.**

   Make **13** or **DRUNK** the row variable and **33** or **CH ATTEND** the column variable. *Press C for column percentages.* Fill in the table.

	WEEKLY	MONTHLY	YEARLY	NEVER
GETS DRUNK	%	%	%	%
NO	%	%	%	%
ABSTAINS	%	%	%	%

V = _____ Prob. = _____

Is the difference statistically significant? **(circle one)**   YES   NO

Is the hypothesis supported or rejected? **(circle one)**   SUPPORTED   REJECTED

Does this result surprise you? Explain.

Part III - *DRUGS AND ALCOHOL*

Worksheets - Exercise 6

6. The hypothesis is: **Single people are more likely than married people to get drunk.**

    Make **13** or **DRUNK** the row variable and **36** or **SINGLE/MAR** the column variable. *Press C for column percentages.* Fill in the table.

	SINGLE	MARRIED
GETS DRUNK	%	%
NO	%	%
ABSTAINS	%	%

    V = _____ Prob. = _____

    Is the difference statistically significant? **(circle one)**   YES   NO

    Is the hypothesis supported or rejected? **(circle one)**   SUPPORTED   REJECTED

    Does this result surprise you? Explain.

Name: **Worksheets** - Exercise 6

7. The hypothesis is: **The more sex partners people have had in the past year, the more likely they are to get drunk.**

   Make **13** or **DRUNK** the row variable and **20** or **SEX PARTNR** the column variable. *Press C for column percentages. Fill in the table.*

	NONE	ONE	2 OR MORE
GETS DRUNK	%	%	%
NO	%	%	%
ABSTAINS	%	%	%

   V = _____ Prob. = _____

   Is the difference statistically significant? (circle one)   YES   NO

   Is the hypothesis supported or rejected? (circle one)   SUPPORTED   REJECTED

   Now examine this relationship separately for males and females.

   Make **13** or **DRUNK** the row variable and **20** or **SEX PARTNR** the column variable, and make **21** or **SEX** the control variable. *Press C for column percentages. Fill in the table.*

MALES

	NONE	ONE	2 OR MORE
GETS DRUNK	%	%	%
NO	%	%	%
ABSTAINS	%	%	%

V = _____ Prob. = _____

Is the difference statistically significant? (circle one)   YES   NO

Is the hypothesis supported or rejected? (circle one)   SUPPORTED   REJECTED

Part III - *DRUGS AND ALCOHOL*

Worksheets - Exercise 6

FEMALES

	NONE	ONE	2 OR MORE
GETS DRUNK	%	%	%
NO	%	%	%
ABSTAINS	%	%	%

V = _____ Prob. = _____

Is the difference statistically significant? (circle one)   YES   NO

Is the hypothesis supported or rejected? (circle one)   SUPPORTED   REJECTED

Compare the values of V. Is the correlation higher among males or females? (circle one)   MALES   FEMALES

Why do you suppose this difference exists?

EXERCISE 7: Cocaine and Alcohol Abuse: State Rates

Open the **FIFTYC** data file and go to the red **STATISTICAL ANALYSIS MENU**. *Place* the highlight on **E. Mapping Variables** and *press <ENTER>*. Now the screen asks you for the name or number of the variable you wish to map. *Type* **65** or **COKE USERS** and *press <ENTER>*. What you are mapping is the official, estimated rate of cocaine addiction per 1,000 population.

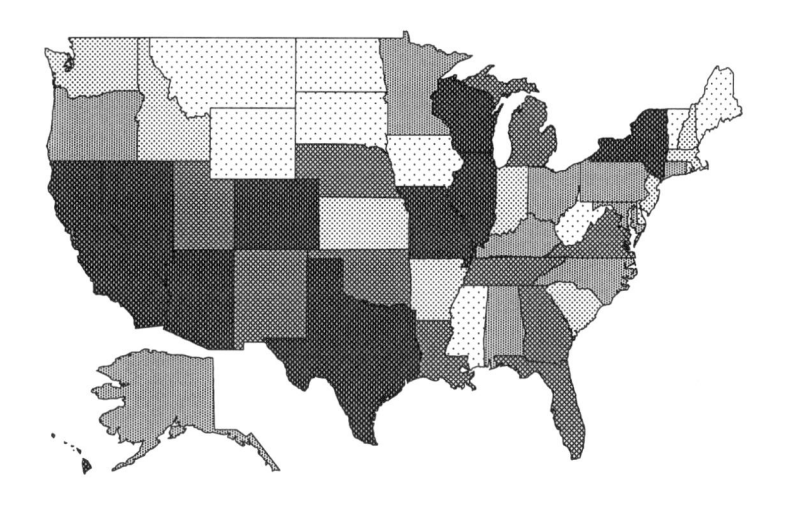

1992: Cocaine addicts per 1,000

Notice that there is a modest southwestern tilt to cocaine addiction rates. *Type N (for Name)* to see which state has the highest rate of cocaine addiction.

Nevada is highest with a rate of 24.9 per 1,000 population. *Press the down arrow to see the next highest state.* New York is just barely lower than Nevada with a rate of 24.5. Another way to present these rates is that of every 200 residents of Nevada and New York, about 5 are addicted to cocaine. Keep in mind, however, that the rate is based on all residents, including infants and small children. So, the rate among people in their late teens and older is probably a good deal higher than this.

Press D (for Distribution) and all 50 states will appear on the screen, ranked from high to low. Vermont, the Dakotas, and Montana have the lowest rates.

Press <ENTER> twice to clear the screen and you will be ready to create another map. Map **67** or **LIQUOR**. What you are mapping is the amount of alcoholic beverages consumed annually by the average person 18 and older. The amount is reported in gallons.

Part III - DRUGS AND ALCOHOL

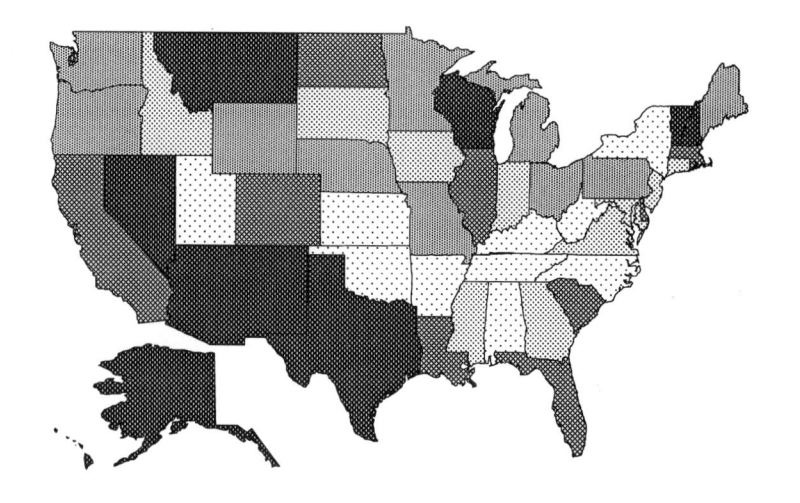

Exercise 7

1989: Gallons of alcoholic beverages consumed per person 18 and over

This map only modestly resembles the map of cocaine addition, although Nevada is the highest here too. *Type N (for Name)* to see that the average person in Nevada, age 18 and older, bought 60.69 gallons of alcoholic beverages. *Press the down arrow to see the next highest state.* New Hampshire is just barely lower than Nevada — people there bought 52.00 gallons. *Press D (for Distribution)* and all 50 states will appear on the screen, ranked from high to low. Utah is lowest with 21.47 gallons. This helps us notice that there is substantial variation between cocaine addiction rates and alcohol sales — since Utah was seventeenth from the top on cocaine addiction.

Switch to **F. Scatterplot**. Use **65** or **COKE USERS** as the dependent variable and **67** or **LIQUOR** as the independent variable.

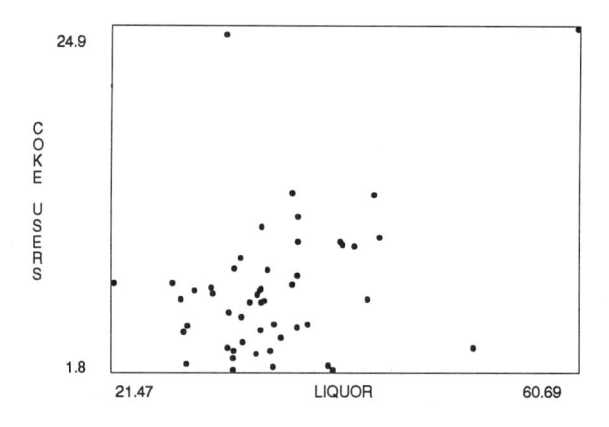

When the scatterplot appears you will discover that the correlation between these two variables is 0.378 and Prob. = 0.003. The correlation is significant.

Return to **E. Mapping Variables**. Map **68** or **BEER**. What you are mapping is the amount of beer purchased annually by the average person 18 and older. The amount is reported in gallons.

82. CRIMINOLOGY - *An Introduction Using MicroCase*

Exercise 7

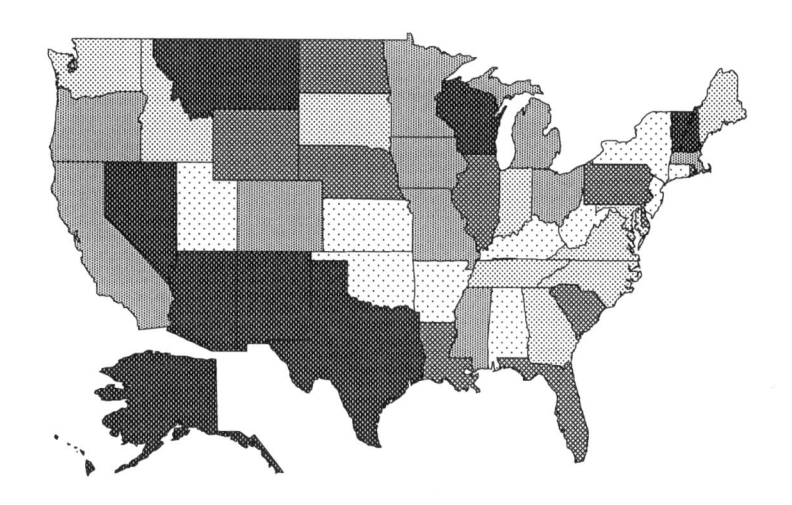

1989: Gallons of beer consumed per person 18 and over

This map closely resembles the map of alcohol purchases. That's because the major portion of alcohol consumption is in the form of beer — in no state does beer make up less than 80 percent. *Press D (for Distribution)* and all 50 states will appear on the screen, ranked from high to low. Nevada and New Hampshire still lead the list while Arkansas, Kentucky, Oklahoma and Utah again make up the bottom four.

Press <ENTER> twice to clear the screen and you will be ready to create another map. Map **105** or **CIRRHOSIS** and *press <ENTER>*. You already have examined this map at the end of Exercise 6. This is the death rate for cirrhosis of the liver, which typically is caused by years of acute alcoholism.

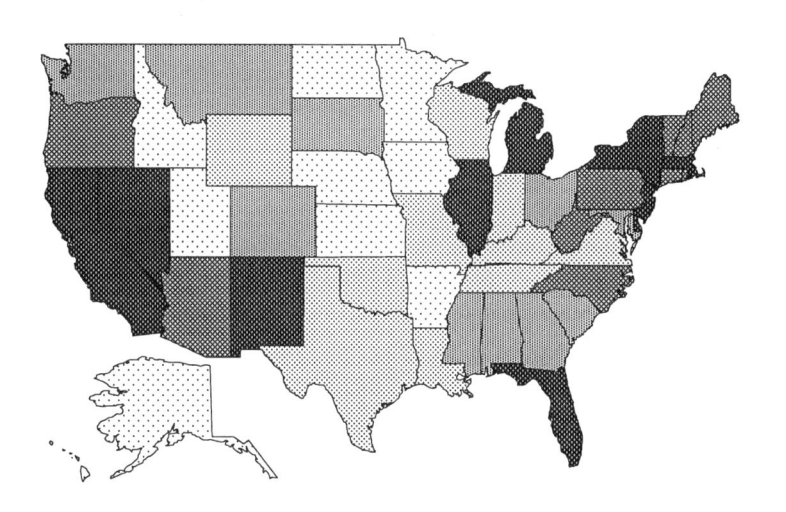

1986: Deaths from cirrhosis of the liver per 100,000

This map only modestly resembles the maps of alcohol and of beer purchases, and in fact looks somewhat more like the map of cocaine addiction. *Type N (for Name)* to see that in Nevada, 17.6 persons per 100,000 died of cirrhosis. *Press the down arrow to see the next highest state.* New York is next highest with a rate of 15.2. *Press D (for Distribution)* and

Part III - *DRUGS AND ALCOHOL*   83.

Exercise 7

all 50 states will appear on the screen, ranked from high to low. Utah is lowest with a rate of 5.3.

Switch to **G. Correlation**. Use the following variables in a correlation matrix: **65** or **COKE USERS**, **67** or **LIQUOR**, and **105** or **CIRRHOSIS**. The results will be these:

	COKE USERS	LIQUOR	CIRRHOSIS
COKE USERS	1.000	0.378**	0.489**
LIQUOR	0.378**	1.000	0.411**
CIRRHOSIS	0.489**	0.411**	1.000

The most interesting thing about these correlations is that, although all are significant, cirrhosis is more highly correlated with cocaine addiction rates than with alcohol consumption, despite the fact that it is liquor, not cocaine, that causes the disease. Let's see why.

Use the following variables in a correlation matrix: **105** or **CIRRHOSIS**, **70** or **% WINE**, **71** or **% BEER**, and **26** or **% METROPOL**. The results will be these:

	CIRRHOSIS	% WINE	% BEER	% METROPOL
CIRRHOSIS	1.000	0.514**	-0.516**	0.449**
% WINE	0.514**	1.000	-0.944**	0.530**
% BEER	-0.516**	-0.944**	1.000	-0.504**
% METROPOL	0.449**	0.530**	-0.504**	1.000

Cirrhosis seems to better reflect *what form of alcohol* is consumed, and *where*. The cirrhosis rate is high in metropolitan states where a lot of wine is consumed. It is low where beer predominates. It is perhaps worth noting that alcoholic derelicts in cities often are called "winos" from their dependence on cheap wine. But the more important fact is the "dark side" of urban sophistication, alluded to in Exercise 1. That is, acute alcoholism is more common where affluent people appreciate fine wines and subscribe to *Gourmet* and *Cosmopolitan*, where income and rents are high, and where also the rates are high for dropping out of school and for contracting a sexually transmitted disease.

Your turn.

Name: _____ **_Worksheets_** - Exercise 7

> *Workbook exercises and software are copyrighted. Copying is prohibited by law.*

1. The hypothesis is: **States that spend more money per student on drug awareness education will have lower rates of cocaine addiction.**

   Open the **FIFTYC** data file and *select* the scatterplot function. Create the following scatterplot:

   Dependent variable: **65** or **COKE USERS**
   Independent variable: **66** or **DRUG ED**

   Write in the long label for **66** or **DRUG ED**: (Press X to see it) _____

   _____

   _____

   What is the correlation coefficient?   r = _____

   Is this a positive or negative correlation? (circle one)   POS   NEG

   Is the difference statistically significant? (circle one)   YES   NO

   Is the hypothesis supported or rejected? (circle one)   SUPPORTED   REJECTED

   Can you suggest reasons for this particular outcome?

Part III - *DRUGS AND ALCOHOL*

Worksheets - Exercise 7

2. The hypothesis is: **States with more poor people, as reflected by the percent of all households receiving aid to families with dependent children (AFDC), will have higher rates of cocaine addiction.**

    Create the following scatterplot:

    Dependent variable: **65** or **COKE USERS**
    Independent variable: **35** or **% AFDC**

    What is the correlation coefficient? r = _____

    Is the difference statistically significant? (circle one)　　　　　　YES　NO

    Is the hypothesis supported or rejected? (circle one)　　SUPPORTED　REJECTED

    Were you surprised by this particular outcome? Explain.

Name: *Worksheets* - Exercise 7

3. The hypothesis is: **States with larger African-American populations will have higher rates of cocaine addiction.**

   Create the following scatterplot:

   Dependent variable: **65** or **COKE USERS**
   Independent variable: **19** or **%AFRIC-A**

   What is the correlation coefficient?   r = _____

   Is the difference statistically significant? (circle one)   YES   NO

   Is the hypothesis supported or rejected? (circle one)   SUPPORTED   REJECTED

   Were you surprised by this particular outcome? Explain.

Part III - *DRUGS AND ALCOHOL*   87.

Worksheets - Exercise 7

4. The hypothesis is: **States with high rates of school dropouts will have higher rates of cocaine addiction.**

    Create the following scatterplot:

    Dependent variable: **65** or **COKE USERS**
    Independent variable: **49** or **% DROPOUTS**

    What is the correlation coefficient? r = _____

    Is the difference statistically significant? (circle one) YES NO

    Is the hypothesis supported or rejected? (circle one) SUPPORTED REJECTED

    Were you surprised by this particular outcome? Explain.

Name: _____ **Worksheets** - Exercise 7

5. *Switch to* **G. Correlation**. Use the variables **65** or **COKE USERS**, **67** or **LIQUOR**, and **56** or **PLAYBOY** and fill in the correlation matrix:

	COKE USERS	LIQUOR	PLAYBOY
COKE USERS			
LIQUOR			
PLAYBOY			

What is the correlation between cocaine addiction and Playboy? _____

Is it significant? (circle one) YES   NO

What is the correlation between liquor purchases and Playboy? _____

Is it significant? (circle one) YES   NO

Is the impact of Playboy circulation rates greater on cocaine addiction or on alcohol consumption? (circle one)   COCAINE   ALCOHOL

Were you surprised by this particular outcome? Explain.

Part III - *DRUGS AND ALCOHOL*

Worksheets - Exercise 7

6. Use the variables **65** or **COKE USERS**, **67** or **LIQUOR**, and **8** or **HOMICIDE** and fill in the correlation matrix:

	COKE USERS	LIQUOR	HOMICIDE
COKE USERS			
LIQUOR			
HOMICIDE			

What is the correlation between cocaine addiction and homicide? _____

Is the difference statistically significant? **(circle one)**   YES NO

What is the correlation between liquor purchases and homicide? _____

Is the difference statistically significant? **(circle one)**   YES NO

Which has the greater impact on homicide rates: rates of cocaine addiction or of alcohol consumption? **(circle one)**   COCAINE   ALCOHOL

Were you surprised by this particular outcome? Explain.

Name: _____   **Worksheets** - Exercise 7

7. Use the variables **65** or **COKE USERS**, **67** or **LIQUOR**, and **10** or **ROBBERY** and fill in the correlation matrix:

	COKE USERS	LIQUOR	ROBBERY
COKE USERS			
LIQUOR			
ROBBERY			

What is the correlation between cocaine addiction and the robbery rate? _____

Is the difference statistically significant? (circle one)   YES   NO

What is the correlation between liquor purchases and the robbery rate? _____

Significant? (circle one)   YES   NO

Which has the greater impact on robbery rates: rates of cocaine addiction or of alcohol consumption? (circle one)   COCAINE   ALCOHOL

Were you surprised by this particular outcome? Explain.

Part III - *DRUGS AND ALCOHOL*

Worksheets - Exercise 7

8. Use the variables **65** or **COKE USERS**, **67** or **LIQUOR**, and **11** or **ASSAULT** and fill in the correlation matrix:

	COKE USERS	LIQUOR	ASSAULT
COKE USERS			
LIQUOR			
ASSAULT			

What is the correlation between cocaine addiction and the assault rate? _____

Significant? **(circle one)** YES NO

What is the correlation between liquor purchases and the assault rate? _____

Significant? **(circle one)** YES NO

Which has the greater impact on assault rates: rates of cocaine addiction or of alcohol consumption? **(circle one)** COCAINE ALCOHOL

Were you surprised by this particular outcome? Explain.

EXERCISE 8: Alcohol and Drugs in High School

In Exercise 3 we discovered that drinking and marijuana use were quite high among high school seniors — about one in four had *not* had a drink in the past month and only half had never used marijuana. Now it's time to ask: Who drinks and/or smokes marijuana, and who doesn't?

Open the **HISCHOOL** data file. Select **B. Tabular Statistics**. Now the screen asks you for the name or number of the row variable. *Type* **4** or **MARIJUANA** and *press <ENTER>*. Make **3** or **DRINK/30** the column variable. When the screen asks for a control variable, simply *press <ENTER>*. When the screen asks for a subset variable, simply *press <ENTER>*. When this table appears on the screen *press C for column percentages*.

	NEVER	1 OR 2	3 OR MORE
NEVER	72.8	55.5	29.3
1 OR 2	8.9	14.3	10.7
SOMETIMES	10.1	16.9	22.6
OFTEN	8.1	13.3	37.4

Here we see that there is a tendency for these students to do both or neither. Of those who had not had a drink during the past month, almost three-fourths (72.8%) had never tried marijuana. Of those who had three or more drinks during the past month, 70 percent had used marijuana and more than a third had done so often.

The hypothesis is: **Among seniors, males are more likely than females to drink frequently and to use marijuana.**

Make **3** or **DRINK/30** the row variable, and select **5** or **SEX** as the column variable. When the table appears on the screen *press C for column percentages*.

	MALE	FEMALE
NEVER	24.7	32.4
1 OR 2	24.1	32.6
3 OR MORE	51.2	34.9

Half of the males had drunk alcohol on three or more occasions that month, compared to only about a third of the females. This is about the same magnitude of difference as in the proportion of adult males and females who drink (see Exercise 6).

Exercise 8

Make **4** or **MARIJUANA** the row variable, and select **5** or **SEX** as the column variable. When the table appears on the screen *press C for column percentages*.

	MALE	FEMALE
NEVER	46.6	53.1
1 OR 2	10.9	11.4
SOMETIMES	16.9	17.3
OFTEN	25.6	18.2

Here the gender differences are even smaller, albeit significant and in the direction predicted by the hypothesis.

The hypothesis is: **Among seniors, non-Hispanic whites are LESS likely than members of minority racial and ethnic groups to drink frequently.**

Make **3** or **DRINK/30** the row variable, and select **6** or **RACE/ETH** as the column variable. When the table appears on the screen *press C for column percentages*.

	WHITE	AFRICAN-AM	HISP-AMER	ASIAN-AMER
NEVER	20.9	40.3	30.9	42.8
1 OR 2	24.8	31.9	32.9	29.8
3 OR MORE	54.3	27.8	36.1	27.5

Wrong! Non-Hispanic white seniors are the group most likely to drink, and to drink often. The differences are very substantial. African-Americans and Asian-Americans are least likely to drink.

These findings match those for the general adult population, at least in terms of differences between whites and African-Americans. Despite widely held stereotypes to the contrary, studies always show that non-Hispanic whites are far more likely to drink than are members of other major racial and ethnic groups.

But what about drugs? The impression gained from the evening news and from "police shows" on TV is that drug use is concentrated among racial and ethnic minorities. Let's see.

The hypothesis is: **Among seniors, non-Hispanic whites are LESS likely than members of minority racial and ethnic groups to use marijuana.**

Make **4** or **MARIJUANA** the row variable, and select **6** or **RACE/ETH** as the column variable. When the table appears on the screen *press C for column percentages*.

Exercise 8

	WHITE	AFRICAN-AM	HISP-AMER	ASIAN-AMER
NEVER	44.4	55.9	55.0	58.0
1 OR 2	10.1	12.3	12.2	10.4
SOMETIMES	18.5	16.4	15.2	17.8
OFTEN	26.9	15.4	17.6	13.8

Wrong again! Here too non-Hispanic whites are the group by far the most likely to use marijuana — 55.5 percent had done so, while about that same percentage of those in the other three racial and ethnic groups had not done so.

Before you are finished with these lab exercises you will encounter many major instances, such as these, when things that "everyone knows" just aren't so.

Folk wisdom has it that "the Devil finds work for idle hands." Phrased by modern control theories of crime and deviance this becomes the proposition that to the extent that people have a lot of spare time on their hands, they will tend to get into trouble. An indicator that people have a lot of spare time is this item:

"How often do you just drive or ride around (alone or with friends)?"

Make **3** or **DRINK/30** the row variable, and select **14** or **CRUISING** as the column variable. When the table appears on the screen *press C for column percentages*.

	DAILY	1-2 WEEK	NOT OFTEN
NEVER	21.8	23.7	36.2
1 OR 2	24.9	28.7	30.4
3 OR MORE	53.3	47.7	33.5

The hypothesis is supported. More than half of those who cruised every day had drunk on three or more occasions during the past month, whereas only a third of those who didn't cruise did so. Here we must worry about gender effects. Males are more likely both to drink and to cruise. So it is advisable for us to examine the relationship between "cruising and boozing" separately for males and females.

Make **3** or **DRINK/30** the row variable, and select **14** or **CRUISING** as the column variable. When the screen asks for a control variable select **5** or **SEX**. When the table appears on the screen *press C for column percentages*.

Part III - *DRUGS AND ALCOHOL*

Exercise 8

MALES

	DAILY	1-2 WEEK	NOT OFTEN
NEVER	17.0	21.8	31.0
1 OR 2	21.0	24.4	25.3
3 OR MORE	62.0	53.7	43.7

This table includes only males. Here too we see that cruising is strongly related to drinking — nearly two-thirds of those who cruised daily had taken drinks on three or more occasions during the past month.

Press <ENTER> to move to the table for females. When the table appears on the screen *press C for column percentages.*

FEMALES

	DAILY	1-2 WEEK	NOT OFTEN
NEVER	26.7	25.4	39.7
1 OR 2	29.1	32.5	33.8
3 OR MORE	44.2	42.1	26.5

This table includes only females. Cruising influences drinking behavior among females too — although the major effect is between those who seldom cruise and others, since those who cruise daily are not much more apt to drink than are those who cruise once or twice a week.

Your turn.

Name: _____   **WORKSHEETS** - Exercise 8

> Workbook exercises and software are copyrighted. Copying is prohibited by law.

Open the **HISCHOOL** data file and select the Tabular Statistics function.

1. The hypothesis is: **Poverty is a major cause of student drug and alcohol use; therefore students from privileged backgrounds will be less likely to drink, to drink often, or to use marijuana.**

   FAMILY SES is a measure based on the family's income and on occupational status (based on the family member with the highest occupational status). Each category includes about a quartile (25 percent) of the sample.

   Make **3** or **DRINK/30** the row variable and **10** or **FAMILY SES** the column variable. Press C for column percentages. Fill in the table.

	LOWEST Q	QUARTILE 2	QUARTILE 3	HIGHEST Q
NEVER	%	%	%	%
1 OR 2	%	%	%	%
3 OR MORE	%	%	%	%

   V = _____   Prob. = _____

   Is the difference statistically significant? (circle one)   YES   NO

   Is the hypothesis supported or rejected? (circle one)   SUPPORTED   REJECTED

   Make **4** or **MARIJUANA** the row variable and **10** or **FAMILY SES** the column variable. Press C for column percentages. Fill in the table.

	LOWEST Q	QUARTILE 2	QUARTILE 3	HIGHEST Q
NEVER	%	%	%	%
1 OR 2	%	%	%	%
SOMETIMES	%	%	%	%
OFTEN	%	%	%	%

   V = _____   Prob. = _____

   Is the difference statistically significant? (circle one)   YES   NO

   Is the hypothesis supported or rejected? (circle one)   SUPPORTED   REJECTED

Part III - *DRUGS AND ALCOHOL*

Worksheets - Exercise 8

Do these results surprise you? Explain.

2. We have seen that cruising is related to drinking and using marijuana. Another measure of free time is:

   "How often do you spend time visiting with friends at a local gathering place?"

   The hypothesis is: **The more time students spend "hanging out," the more apt they are to drink and to use marijuana.**

   Make **3** or **DRINK/30** the row variable and **15** or **HANGIN'OUT** the column variable. *Press C for column percentages.* Fill in the table.

	DAILY	1-2 WEEK	NOT OFTEN
NEVER	%	%	%
1 OR 2	%	%	%
3 OR MORE	%	%	%

   V = _____ Prob. = _____

   Is the difference statistically significant? **(circle one)**   YES   NO

   Is the hypothesis supported or rejected? **(circle one)**   SUPPORTED   REJECTED

Name: _____ *Worksheets* - Exercise 8

Make **4** or **MARIJUANA** the row variable and **15** or **HANGIN'OUT** the column variable. *Press C for column percentages.* Fill in the table.

	DAILY	1-2 WEEK	NOT OFTEN
NEVER	%	%	%
1 OR 2	%	%	%
SOMETIMES	%	%	%
OFTEN	%	%	%

V = _____ Prob. = _____

Is the difference statistically significant? (circle one)   YES   NO

Is the hypothesis supported or rejected? (circle one)   SUPPORTED   REJECTED

3. If having a lot of free time to cruise and hang out is conducive to drinking and marijuana use, shouldn't participation in varsity sports have the opposite effect of keeping students too busy to get in trouble?

    The hypothesis is: **Students who participate in varsity sports will be less likely to drink or to use marijuana.**

    Make **3** or **DRINK/30** the row variable and **18** or **SPORTS?** the column variable. *Press C for column percentages.* Fill in the table.

	NO	VARSITY
NEVER	%	%
1 OR 2	%	%
3 OR MORE	%	%

V = _____ Prob. = _____

Is the difference statistically significant? (circle one)   YES   NO

Is the hypothesis supported or rejected? (circle one)   SUPPORTED   REJECTED

It might be wise to examine the effects of sports participation separately for males and females.

Part III - *DRUGS AND ALCOHOL*

Worksheets - Exercise 8

Make **3** or **DRINK/30** the row variable and **18** or **SPORTS?** the column variable. Make **5** or **SEX** the control variable. *Press C for column percentages.* Fill in the table.

MALES

	NO	VARSITY
NEVER	%	%
1 OR 2	%	%
3 OR MORE	%	%

V = _____ Prob. = _____

Is the difference statistically significant? (circle one)   YES   NO

Is the hypothesis supported or rejected? (circle one)   SUPPORTED   REJECTED

Press <ENTER> twice to move to the table for females. When the table appears on the screen *press C for column percentages.*

FEMALES

	NO	VARSITY
NEVER	%	%
1 OR 2	%	%
3 OR MORE	%	%

V = _____ Prob. = _____

Is the difference statistically significant? (circle one)   YES   NO

Is the hypothesis supported or rejected? (circle one)   SUPPORTED   REJECTED

Make **4** or **MARIJUANA** the row variable and **18** or **SPORTS?** the column variable. *Press C for column percentages.* Fill in the table.

Name: *Worksheets* - Exercise 8

	NO	VARSITY
NEVER	%	%
1 OR 2	%	%
SOMETIMES	%	%
OFTEN	%	%

V = _____ Prob. = _____

Is the difference statistically significant? **(circle one)**   YES   NO

Is the hypothesis supported or rejected? **(circle one)**   SUPPORTED   REJECTED

Here too it would be wise to examine the effects of sports participation separately for males and females.

Make **4** or **MARIJUANA** the row variable and **18** or **SPORTS** the column variable. Make **5** or **SEX** the control variable. *Press C for column percentages.* Fill in the table.

MALES

	NO	VARSITY
NEVER	%	%
1 OR 2	%	%
SOMETIMES	%	%
OFTEN	%	%

V = _____ Prob. = _____

Is the difference statistically significant? **(circle one)**   YES   NO

Is the hypothesis supported or rejected? **(circle one)**   SUPPORTED   REJECTED

Press <ENTER> twice to move to the table for females. When the table appears on the screen *press C for column percentages.*

Part III - *DRUGS AND ALCOHOL*

Worksheets - Exercise 8

FEMALES

	NO	VARSITY
NEVER	%	%
1 OR 2	%	%
SOMETIMES	%	%
OFTEN	%	%

V = _____ Prob. = _____

Is the difference statistically significant? **(circle one)**   YES   NO

Is the hypothesis supported or rejected? **(circle one)**   SUPPORTED   REJECTED

Why do you think varsity sports participation has different effects for males and females?

EXERCISE 9: Drinking and Doing Drugs in College

We have seen that alcohol and drug use among high school seniors doesn't always conform to widely held stereotypes. Now let's see if similar patterns hold for college students.

The hypothesis is: **There is a sequence in drug use: People seldom use marijuana who do not also drink alcohol.**

Open the **COLLEGEC** data file and select **B. Tabular Statistics**. Now the screen asks you for the name or number of the row variable. *Type* **6** or **POT NOW** and *press* *<ENTER>*. Make **4** or **DRINK?** the column variable. When the screen asks for a control variable, simply *press <ENTER>*. When the screen asks for a subset variable, simply *press <ENTER>*. When this table appears on the screen *press C for column percentages*.

	DRINK NOW	ABSTAIN NOW
PAST YEAR	43.8	11.3
NO	56.3	88.7

Here is strong support for the hypothesis. Only 11.3 percent of students who now abstain from alcohol have used marijuana during the past year. But, of students who drink, more than 4 out of 10 have used marijuana in the past year. *Press S (for Statistics)*. Prob. = 0.000.

Press <ENTER> twice and you will be ready to run a new table.

The hypothesis is: **Students will seldom use cocaine without also using marijuana.**

Make **7** or **COKE NOW** the row variable, and select **6** or **POT NOW** as the column variable. When the table appears on the screen *press C for column percentages*.

	PAST YEAR	NO
PAST YEAR	12.8	0.6
NOT	87.2	99.4

Once again the hypothesis is very strongly supported. Of those who have smoked marijuana in the past year, 12.8 percent also have used cocaine whereas only 0.6 of those who did not smoke marijuana used cocaine. However, because so few students in this sample did use cocaine during the previous year (only 25 did) it will not be feasible to analyze who they were — which illustrates why it is so valuable to have very large samples when wishing to study a relatively rare phenomenon.

Press <ENTER> and you will be ready to run a new table.

Part III - DRUGS AND ALCOHOL

Exercise 9

The hypothesis is: **Males are more likely than females to currently drink alcohol.**

Make **4** or **DRINK?** the row variable, and select **10** or **SEX** as the column variable. When the table appears on the screen *press C for column percentages.*

	FEMALE	MALE
DRINK NOW	70.9	65.4
ABSTAIN	29.1	34.6

Surprise! At this university it appears that females are more likely to drink. However, *press S (for Statistics).* Prob. = 0.176. The difference is not statistically significant.

So, what about marijuana?

Make **6** or **POT NOW** the row variable, and select **10** or **SEX** as the column variable. When the table appears on the screen *press C for column percentages.*

	FEMALE	MALE
PAST YEAR	31.5	35.5
NO	68.5	64.5

Press S (for Statistics). Prob. = 0.326. Nor is this difference statistically significant.

In Exercise 6 we found that in the general public men were more likely than women to drink. In Exercise 8 we found that among high school seniors males were more likely than females to drink and to use marijuana. But here, among college students, the gender differences do not turn up. Is it possible that there is something about college that washes out gender differences in the tendency to drink and to use drugs?

To find out, *open* the **NORC** data file and select **B. Tabular Statistics** from the **STATISTICAL ANALYSIS MENU**. Now the screen asks you for the name or number of the row variable. *Type* **12** or **DRINK?** and *press <ENTER>*. Make **21** or **SEX** the column variable. When the screen asks for a control variable, use **28** or **EDUCATION**. When this first table appears on the screen *press C for column percentages.*

UNDER 12

	MALE	FEMALE
USE ALC	62.8	49.6
ABSTAIN	37.2	50.4

This table is limited to persons who did not finish high school. Among them we see a substantial gender difference. *Press S (for Statistics)*. Prob. = 0.000. And it is highly significant. *Press <ENTER> twice* to move to the next table. When the table appears on the screen *press C for column percentages*.

HS GRAD.

	MALE	FEMALE
USE ALC	76.9	64.4
ABSTAINS	23.1	35.6

This table is limited to persons who graduated from high school. Among them we also see a substantial gender difference. *Press S (for Statistics)*. Prob. = 0.000. And it is highly significant.

Press <ENTER> twice to move to the next table. When the table appears on the screen *press C for column percentages*.

SOME COLL

	MALE	FEMALE
USE ALC	76.7	74.6
ABSTAINS	23.3	25.4

This table is limited to persons who attended college. And suddenly, the gender difference has disappeared. *Press S (for Statistics)*. Prob. = 0.539.

Press <ENTER> twice to move to the next table. When the table appears on the screen *press C for column percentages*.

COLL GRAD

	MALE	FEMALE
USE ALC	78.9	74.6
ABSTAINS	21.1	25.4

This table is limited to persons who graduated from college. Here too the gender difference has disappeared. *Press S (for Statistics)*. Prob. = 0.319.

So, now we can have considerable confidence in our previous findings that there were no gender differences in our sample of college students, since gender differences do not hold in the general population for persons who went to college: There *is* something about college that equalizes the tendency for males and females to drink.

Part III - *DRUGS AND ALCOHOL*

Exercise 9

Open the **COLLEGEC** data file and select **B. Tabular Statistics**.

In Exercises 6 and 8 we found that non-Hispanic whites were substantially more likely to drink and to use marijuana than were members of racial and ethnic minorities. In this sample there are insufficient numbers of African-American and Hispanic-American students for separate analysis. There are, however, a sufficient number of Asian-Americans.

Make **4** or **DRINK?** the row variable, and select **11** or **WH/ASIAN** as the column variable. When the table appears on the screen *press C for column percentages*.

	WHITE	ASIAN
DRINK NOW	75.0	52.5
ABSTAIN	25.0	47.5

Once again whites are the group more likely to drink. *Press S (for Statistics)*. Prob. = 0.000. The difference is highly statistically significant.

So, what about marijuana?

Make **6** or **POT NOW** the row variable, and select **11** or **WH/ASIAN** as the column variable. When the table appears on the screen *press C for column percentages*.

	WHITE	ASIAN
PAST YEAR	37.2	18.4
NO	62.8	81.6

Press S (for Statistics). Prob. = 0.000. This difference also is highly statistically significant.

Your turn.

Name: *Worksheets* - Exercise 9

> *Workbook exercises and software are copyrighted. Copying is prohibited by law.*

Open the **COLLEGEC** data file and select the Tabular Statistics function.

1. The hypothesis is: **Where, and with whom, students live will influence their use of alcohol and drugs.**

    Before beginning to test this hypothesis, examine the following list of student living quarters and rank them from highest (1) to lowest (5) in terms of the percentage of students who will drink. Then assign each a rank for marijuana smoking. You will not be graded on these answers, so go ahead and make your best guesses.

	Rank on drinking	Rank on marijuana
With Parents	_____	_____
Own Apartment	_____	_____
Dorm	_____	_____
Sorority	_____	_____
Fraternity	_____	_____

    Make **4** or **DRINK?** the row variable and **9** or **WHERE LIVE** the column variable. *Press C for column percentages.* Fill in the table.

	WITH PAREN	OWN APARTM	DORM	SORORITY	FRATERNITY
DRINK NOW	%	%	%	%	%
ABSTAIN	%	%	%	%	%

    V = _____   Prob. = _____

    Is the difference statistically significant? (circle one)   YES   NO

    In which living situation are students least likely to drink?   _____

    In which are they most likely to drink?   _____

Part III - *DRUGS AND ALCOHOL*

Worksheets - Exercise 9

Make **5** or **THROW UP?** the row variable and **9** or **WHERE LIVE** the column variable. *Press C for column percentages.* Fill in the table.

	WITH PAREN	OWN APARTM	DORM	SORORITY	FRATERNITY
THROW UP	%	%	%	%	%
NO	%	%	%	%	%

V = _____ Prob. = _____

Is the difference statistically significant? (circle one)   YES   NO

In which living situation are students least likely to have thrown up? _____

In which are they most likely to have thrown up? _____

Make **6** or **POT NOW** the row variable and **9** or **WHERE LIVE** the column variable. *Press C for column percentages.* Fill in the table.

	WITH PAREN	OWN APARTM	DORM	SORORITY	FRATERNITY
PAST YEAR	%	%	%	%	%
NO	%	%	%	%	%

V = _____ Prob. = _____

Is the difference statistically significant? (circle one)   YES   NO

In which living situation are students least likely to have used marijuana? _____

In which are they most likely to have used marijuana? _____

How would you interpret or explain these results?

Name: _____   ***Worksheets*** - Exercise 9

2. The hypothesis is: **Students who work will be less likely currently to use drugs or to drink than students who do not work.**

   Make **6** or **POT NOW** the row variable and **16** or **EMPLOYED?** the column variable. *Press C for column percentages.* Fill in the table.

	EMPLOYED	NOT
PAST YEAR	%	%
NO	%	%

   V = _____ Prob. = _____

   Is the difference statistically significant? **(circle one)**   YES   NO

   Make **4** or **DRINK?** the row variable and **16** or **EMPLOYED?** the column variable. *Press C for column percentages.* Fill in the table.

	EMPLOYED	NOT
DRINK NOW	%	%
ABSTAIN	%	%

   V = _____ Prob. = _____

   Is the difference statistically significant? **(circle one)**   YES   NO

   Is the hypothesis supported or rejected? **(circle one)**   SUPPORTED   REJECTED

   Make **5** or **THROW UP?** the row variable and **16** or **EMPLOYED?** the column variable. *Press C for column percentages.* Fill in the table.

	EMPLOYED	NOT
THROW UP	%	%
NO	%	%

   V = _____ Prob. = _____

   Is the difference statistically significant? **(circle one)**   YES   NO

   Is the hypothesis supported or rejected? **(circle one)**   SUPPORTED   REJECTED

Part III - *DRUGS AND ALCOHOL*

Worksheets - Exercise 9

Do these results surprise you? Explain.

3. The hypothesis is: **Based on what we discovered in earlier exercises, students from higher-income homes will be MORE likely currently to use drugs and alcohol than students from lower-income homes.**

   Make **6** or **POT NOW** the row variable and **12** or **FAMILY $** the column variable. *Press C for column percentages.* Fill in the table.

	BELOW AV.	AVERAGE	ABOVE AV.	FAR ABOVE
PAST YEAR	%	%	%	%
NO	%	%	%	%

   V = _____ Prob. = _____

   Is the difference statistically significant? (circle one)   YES   NO

   Is the hypothesis supported or rejected? (circle one)   SUPPORTED   REJECTED

   Make **4** or **DRINK?** the row variable and **12** or **FAMILY $** the column variable. *Press C for column percentages.* Fill in the table.

	BELOW AV.	AVERAGE	ABOVE AV.	FAR ABOVE
DRINK NOW	%	%	%	%
ABSTAIN	%	%	%	%

   V = _____ Prob. = _____

   Is the difference statistically significant? (circle one)   YES   NO

   Is the hypothesis supported or rejected? (circle one)   SUPPORTED   REJECTED

Name: *Worksheets* - Exercise 9

How would you explain the relationship between privilege and alcohol and drug use?

4. The hypothesis is: **Based on what we discovered in Exercise 6, the more sexual partners students have had, the more likely they are to currently drink alcohol.**

Make **4** or **DRINK?** the row variable and **18** or **SEX PARTNR** the column variable. *Press C for column percentages.* Fill in the table.

	NONE	ONE	2-3	4 OR MORE
DRINK NOW	%	%	%	%
ABSTAIN	%	%	%	%

V = _____ Prob. = _____

Is the difference statistically significant? **(circle one)**   YES   NO

Is the hypothesis supported or rejected? **(circle one)**   SUPPORTED   REJECTED

Next, examine this relationship separately for females and males.

Make **4** or **DRINK?** the row variable and **18** or **SEX PARTNR** the column variable and **10** or **SEX** the control variable. *Press C for column percentages.* Fill in the table.

Worksheets - Exercise 9

FEMALES

	NONE	ONE	2-3	4 OR MORE
DRINK NOW	%	%	%	%
ABSTAIN	%	%	%	%

V = _____ Prob. = _____

Is the difference statistically significant? (circle one)   YES   NO

Is the hypothesis supported or rejected? (circle one)   SUPPORTED   REJECTED

MALES

	NONE	ONE	2-3	4 OR MORE
DRINK NOW	%	%	%	%
ABSTAIN	%	%	%	%

V = _____ Prob. = _____

Is the difference statistically significant? (circle one)   YES   NO

Is the hypothesis supported or rejected? (circle one)   SUPPORTED   REJECTED

Compare the values of V. Is the correlation higher among males or females? (circle one)   MALES   FEMALES

Does this finding agree with results found in Exercise 6? (See the last question.) (circle one)   AGREES   DISAGREES

Why do you suppose this gender difference exists?

PART IV: *PROPERTY CRIME*

Property crimes constitute nearly 9 out of 10 of the crimes included in the official UCR data. In 1990, larceny-thefts accounted for 55 percent of the UCR rate, motor vehicle thefts made up 11 percent, and burglary amounted to 21 percent of the total official crime rate. In the four exercises making up this section we will examine property crime. In Exercise 10 we will analyze victimization data to see who is most likely to be burglarized. In Exercise 11 we will test portions of social disorganization theory as explanations of why people in some parts of the nation are so much more likely to be victims of property crimes. Exercise 12 will focus on self-report data for high school students, and Exercise 13 will examine college students to see who commits property crimes.

EXERCISE 10: Burglary Victims

Unlike other crime rates, the burglary rate has been declining sharply. The burglary rate hit its all-time high in 1980 — the national rate was 1,684 per 100,000 Americans. By 1990 it had fallen to 1,236 — a drop of 27 percent. Before we try to discover *who* gets burglarized, let's examine this huge decline in the rate and see where it has been concentrated.

Open the **FIFTYC** data file and select **E. Mapping Variables**. Now the screen asks you for the name or number of the variable you wish to map. *Type* **102** or **BURGLARY 82** and *press <ENTER>*. This is the official burglary rate for 1982.

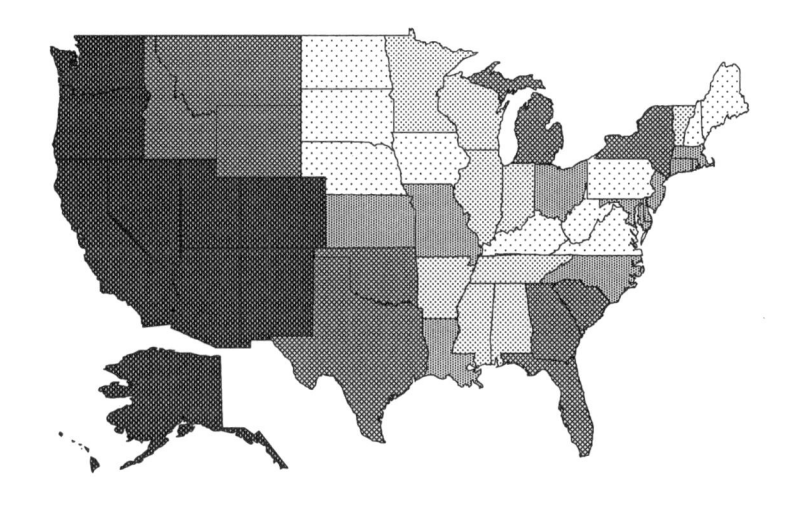

1982: Burglaries per 100,000 population

Notice how extremely high western burglary rates were in 1982. *Type N (for Name)* to see which state had the highest rate. Colorado was highest with a burglary rate of 4,429 per 100,000 population. *Press the down arrow to see the next highest state.* Arizona was just barely lower than Colorado with a rate of 4,361. *Press D (for Distribution)* and all 50 states will appear on the screen, ranked from high to low. Reading down from the top you will see that the top 13 states were all in the Pacific or Mountain region, and only two of the top 15 were southern (Florida and Texas). The Dakotas, where even today many people do not lock

Exercise 10

their doors, had by far the lowest rates — people living in Colorado in 1982 were almost ten times as likely to be burglarized as were people living in North Dakota.

Press <ENTER> twice to clear the screen and you will be ready to create another map. Map **107** or **BURGLARY88**.

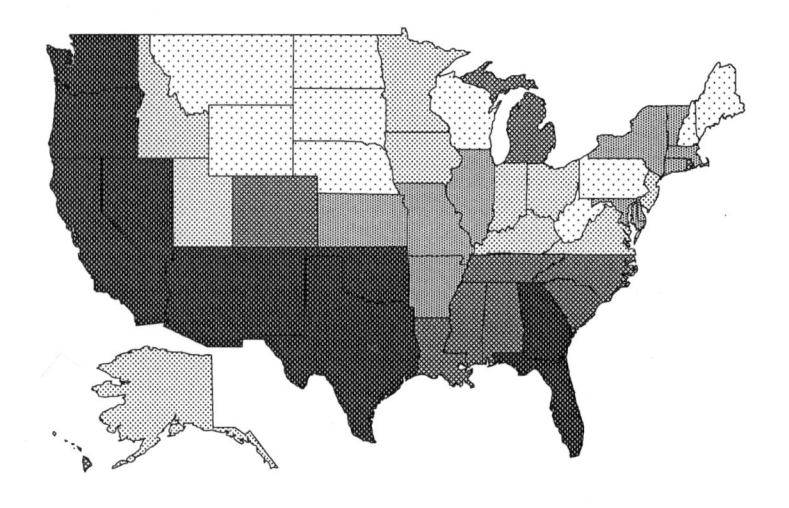

1988: Burglaries per 100,000 population

This map shows that by 1988 burglary wasn't quite so western. *Type N (for Name)* to see which state had the highest rate. Florida was highest with a burglary rate of 2,294 per 100,000 population. Notice that this is a rate only about half that of Colorado's rate only six years earlier. *Press the down arrow to see the next highest state.* Texas was in second place with a rate of 2,157. *Press D (for Distribution)* and all 50 states will appear on the screen, ranked from high to low. Colorado had fallen to 14th place with a rate of only 1,383. Reading down from the top you will see that of the top 15 states (13 of which were western in 1982) only seven are western, while seven are southern.

Press <ENTER> twice to clear the screen and you will be ready to create another map. Map **12** or **BURGLARY**.

The map shows that by 1992 burglary was even less western and more southern. *Type N (for Name)* to see which state had the highest rate. Florida again was highest with a burglary rate of 1,889 per 100,000 population — lower than in 1988. North Carolina has moved to second place with a rate of 1,653 and Texas is now third with a rate of 1,523 per 100,000 population. *Press D (for Distribution)* and all 50 states will appear on the screen, ranked from high to low. Colorado had fallen out of the top 15 with a rate of only 1,091. Reading down from the top you will see that of the top 15 states (seven of which were western in 1988) only four are western, while nine are southern.

Press <ENTER> twice to clear the screen and you will be ready to create another map. Now let's examine the percentage declines from 1982 through 1990. Map **108** or **BUR.CHANGE**.

Exercise 10

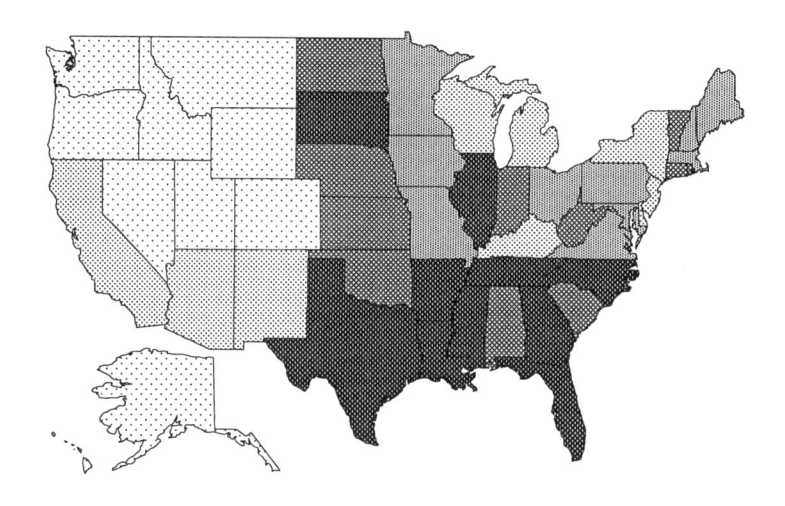

1982-1990: Decline (or increase) in the burglary rate

This map shows the percentage rate of change in each state's burglary rate. Some of the darkest colored states actually had an increase in their burglary rate during this period. *Press D (for distribution)* and all 50 states will appear on the screen, ranked from high to low. North Carolina's rate increased by 14.5 percent, Arkansas' by 11.5 — only southern states showed an increase. The rate for the Dakotas didn't fall by much, but recall how low their rates were to begin with. Now look at the bottom of the list. Wyoming's rate fell by an incredible 433.6 percent, Alaska's by 325.6, Montana's by 323.9, and Utah's by 319.0. The thirteen states with the largest percentage declines in their burglary rates were all in the West — that is, in the Mountain and Pacific regions.

Why did the burglary rates fall so far?

There is no consensus among criminologists. A frequent suggestion is that because the percentage of the population in the age group most likely to commit crimes (individuals in their mid-teens through late twenties) declined a lot during this period, the burglary rate declined too. The trouble with this explanation is that other highly age-related property crimes, such as larceny-theft and auto theft, did not decline, but increased. Between 1980 and 1990 the larceny-theft rate rose by 0.9 percent, from 3,167 offenses per 100,000 to 3,195. During the same period, vehicle thefts rose from 502 per 100,000 to 658, or by 31 percent. If changes in the age composition of the population account for the drop in the burglary rate, these offenses should have declined too.

Another suggestion is that the specific decline in burglary was caused by a substantial increase in home security systems during this period. The idea is that people in the West got tired of their high burglary losses and made their homes much more secure. This may be part of the answer. Unfortunately, no one has assembled good data on improved home security or correlated it with declines in burglary rates.

A third suggestion involves the large increases in the prison populations during this same period. In 1980 there were slightly more than 300,000 prisoners in state and federal prisons and another 200,000 in city and county jails. In 1989 there were nearly 700,000 prisoners in state and federal prisons and more than 300,000 in city and county jails. A primary cause of the increase was not more convictions so much as longer sentences. Since

Part IV - *PROPERTY CRIME*

Exercise 10

the great majority of those in prison for property crimes were convicted of burglary (larceny-theft seldom results in prison time), the average burglar would have been kept out of action for a substantially longer time following each conviction. Criminologists refer to this as an "incapacitation effect." That is, whether or not prison time deters people from committing offenses after their release, people are effectively prevented from committing burglaries while they are behind bars. In 1990 there were about 68,000 more burglars in state and federal prisons than in 1980. In 1990 there were 685,000 fewer *burglaries* than in 1980. If we can assume that each additional burglar in prison was prevented from committing 10 burglaries, the decline is accounted for.

However, despite these suggestive facts, the claim that increases in the "incapacitation" of burglars has played a substantial role in the decline in burglaries remains in the realm of speculation for lack of research on the topic.

But, whatever the reasons for the decline, the question persists: *Who suffers most?*

The hypothesis is: **People in the East and Midwest are less likely to be burglarized than are people elsewhere**.

Open the **NORC** data file and select **Tabular Statistics**. Create a table using **2** or **BURGLED?** as the row variable and **18** or **REGION** as the column variable. The table appears on the screen. *Press C for column percentages.*

	EAST	MIDWEST	SOUTH	MOUNTAIN	PACIFIC
YES	4.7	5.1	5.9	6.3	10.3
NO	95.3	94.9	94.1	93.7	89.7

The hypothesis is supported. *Press S (for Statistics).* Prob. = 0.006. The differences are significant.

Your turn.

Name: _____ **Worksheets** - Exercise 10

> *Workbook exercises and software are copyrighted. Copying is prohibited by law.*

Open the **NORC** data file and select the Tabular Statistics function.

1. The hypothesis is: **Burglars will tend to target the homes of upper-income people**.

    Make **2** or **BURGLED?** the row variable and **26** or **FAMILY $** the column variable. *Press C for column percentages.* Fill in the table.

	UNDER $12K	$12-$23K	$23-$35K	$35-$60K	OVER $60K
YES	%	%	%	%	%
NO	%	%	%	%	%

    V = _____ Prob. = _____

    Is the difference statistically significant? **(circle one)** YES NO

    Is the hypothesis supported or rejected? **(circle one)** SUPPORTED REJECTED

    Does this result surprise you? Explain.

Part IV - *PROPERTY CRIME*

Worksheets - Exercise 10

2. The hypothesis is: **Burglars will tend to target the homes of whites.**

   Make **2** or **BURGLED?** the row variable and **23** or **WH/AF-A** the column variable. *Press C for column percentages.* Fill in the table.

	WHITE	AFRICAN-AM
YES	%	%
NO	%	%

   V = _____ Prob. = _____

   Is the difference statistically significant? (circle one)   YES   NO

   Is the hypothesis supported or rejected? (circle one)   SUPPORTED   REJECTED

   Does this result surprise you? Explain.

Name: **Worksheets** - Exercise 10

3. The hypothesis is: **Burglars will tend to target the homes of single people.**

   Make **2** or **BURGLED?** the row variable and **36** or **SINGLE/MAR** the column variable. *Press C for column percentages.* Fill in the table.

	SINGLE	MARRIED
YES	%	%
NO	%	%

   V = _____ Prob. = _____

   Is the difference statistically significant? (circle one)   YES   NO

   Is the hypothesis supported or rejected? (circle one)   SUPPORTED   REJECTED

   Does this result surprise you? Explain.

Part IV - *PROPERTY CRIME* 119.

Worksheets - Exercise 10

4. The hypothesis is: **Burglars will tend to avoid the homes of gun owners.**

    Make **2** or **BURGLED?** the row variable and **15** or **OWN GUN?** the column variable. *Press C for column percentages.* Fill in the table.

	HAS GUN	NO GUN
YES	%	%
NO	%	%

    V = _____ Prob. = _____

    Is the difference statistically significant? (circle one)   YES   NO

    Is the hypothesis supported or rejected? (circle one)   SUPPORTED   REJECTED

    Does this result surprise you? Explain.

EXERCISE 11: Social Disorganization and Property Crime

Social disorganization theory arose in response to the rapid growth of cities during the 19th century. As rural people flocked to the booming industrial centers, these cities became populated by newcomers and strangers. Moreover, cities became crime-infested and disorderly places. The early sociologists and criminologists linked these two developments. They argued that the moral order is sustained by interpersonal attachments. We obey the norms because we wish to protect our relationships with other people — to retain their good opinion of us. Persons lacking such attachments have much less to risk by being detected in deviant or criminal acts. As cities grew rapidly, human relationships declined — newcomers and strangers lack attachments. As a result, increasingly large numbers of people in rapidly growing places are relatively free to violate norms. Over the years, this has come to be known as the *social disorganization theory of crime*.

In this exercise we are going to see if social disorganization helps to explain geographic variations in property crime, especially burglary and larceny-theft. Since it is one of the oldest criminological theories, we shall begin testing it on data from early in the century.

Open the **FIFTYC** data file and select **E. Mapping Variables**. Now the screen asks you for the name or number of the variable you wish to map. *Type* **89** or **BURGLARY23** and *press* *<ENTER>*. This is based on the number of persons sent to jail or prison for burglary in 1923. This is not the same thing as the number of burglaries known to the police — such UCR rates were not available at this time. However, we shall see that convictions are a good measure of the amount of crime occurring in a community.

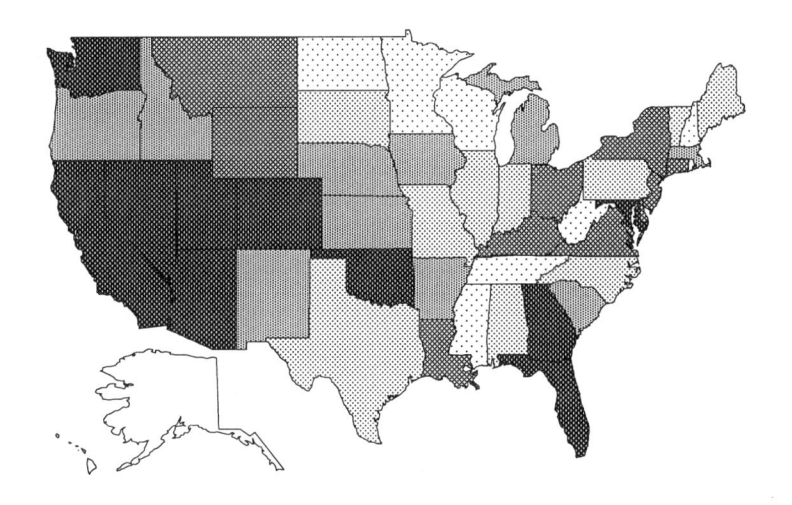

1923: Persons sent up for burglary per 100,000

Notice that burglary tended to be highest in the West and, to a lesser degree, the South in 1923. *Type N (for Name)* to see which state had the highest rate. Nevada was highest with a burglary imprisonment rate of 13 per 100,000 population. *Press the down arrow to see the next highest state.* Arizona was second with a rate of 10.48. *Press D (for Distribution)* and all 50 states will appear on the screen, ranked from high to low. Reading down from the top you will see that of the top 10 states, 6 were all in the Pacific or Mountain

Part IV - *PROPERTY CRIME* 121.

Exercise 11

regions and 4 were southern (Oklahoma, Maryland, Florida, and Georgia). New Hampshire was lowest. Hawaii and Alaska lack rates because they were not states at this time.

Press <ENTER> twice to clear the screen and you will be ready to create another map. Map **90** or **LARCENY 23**. This is based on the number of persons sent to jail or prison in 1923 for larceny-thefts.

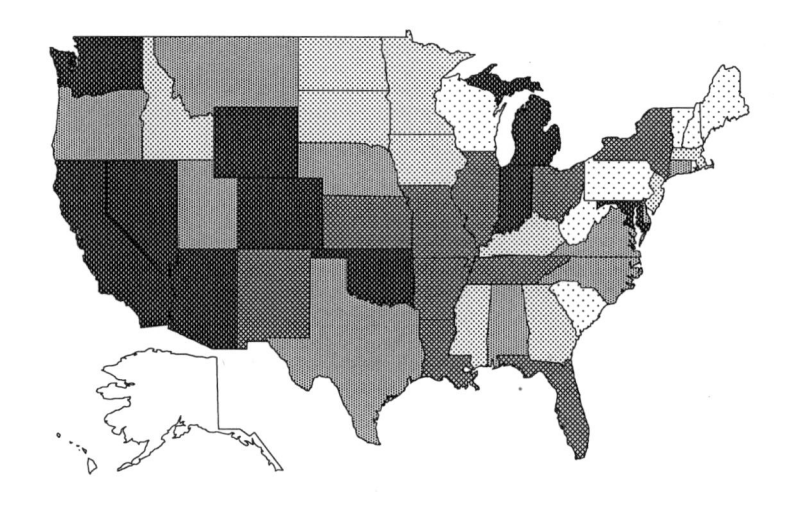

1923: Persons sent up for larceny per 100,000

Larceny tended to be even more western than burglary in 1923. *Type N (for Name)* to see which state had the highest rate. Colorado was highest with a larceny-theft imprisonment rate of 25.43 per 100,000 population. *Press the down arrow to see the next highest state*. Arizona was second with a rate of 21.86. *Press D (for Distribution)* and all 50 states will appear on the screen, ranked from high to low. Reading down from the top you will see that four of the top five states were all in the Pacific or Mountain regions. This time Wisconsin beat out New Hampshire for having the lowest rate.

According to social disorganization theory, states with the highest rates of burglary and larceny ought to be places where social relations have been disorganized by rapid population growth. Let's see.

Press <ENTER> twice to clear the screen and you will be ready to create another map. Map **91** or **POP GO 20**. Here we are mapping the percentage rate of population growth in each state from 1910 through 1920, as calculated by the U.S. Census.

Exercise 11

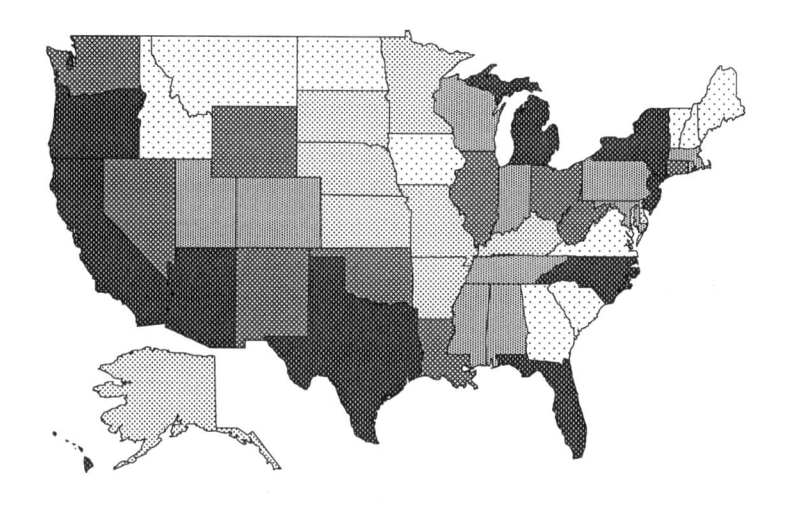

Percent population growth (or decline), 1910-1920

Population growth also tended to be western in 1920. *Type N (for Name)* to see which state had the highest rate. California was highest with a growth rate of 66 percent for the decade. *Press the down arrow to see the next highest state.* Florida was second with a growth rate of 52 percent. *Press D (for Distribution)* and all 50 states will appear on the screen, ranked from high to low.

Press <ENTER> twice to clear the screen and you will be ready to create another map. Map **88** or **%LOCALS 20**. Here we are mapping the percentage of the population in each state in 1920 who were born in that state.

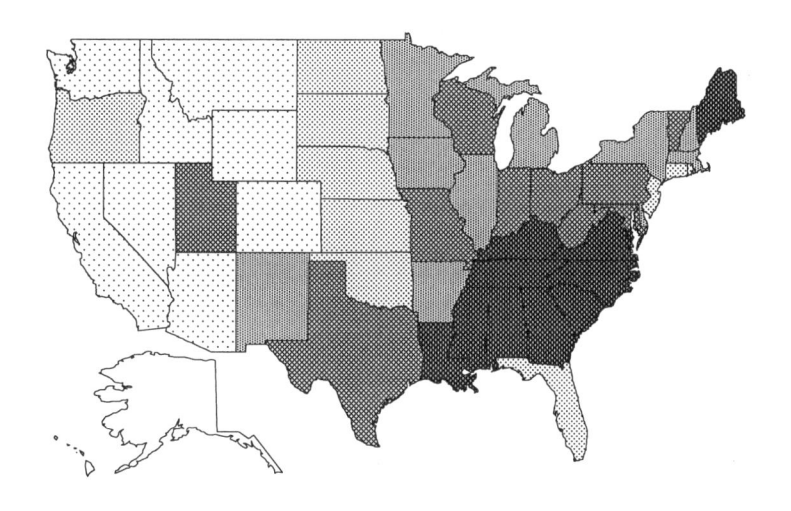

1920: Percent of population born in state of current residence

This variable is the reverse of population growth. Only states lacking migration into the state will have high rates of their population who are native-born. *Press D (for Distribution)* and all fifty states will appear on the screen, ranked from high to low. The Carolinas were highest with 93 percent of their population being native-born in 1920. In fact, the top nine states are in the South.

Part IV - *PROPERTY CRIME*

Exercise 11

It's hard to look at any two maps and guess at the correlation between them unless they are either very alike or very unalike. Here we have a case of maps that are "somewhat" alike. And that's when the correlation coefficient is a vital tool.

Switch to **G. Correlation**. The hypothesis is: **Burglary and larceny convictions will be correlated significantly (positively) with the rate of population growth and negatively with the percent locals**. Use the following variables in a correlation matrix: **91** or **POP GO 20**, **88** or **%LOCALS 20**, **89** or **BURGLARY23**, and **90** or **LARCENY23**. The results will be these:

	POP GO 20	%LOCALS 20	BURGLARY23	LARCENY23
POP GO 20	1.000	-0.235	0.334*	0.429**
%LOCALS 20	-0.235	1.000	-0.484**	-0.441**
BURGLARY23	0.334*	-0.484**	1.000	0.665**
LARCENY 23	0.429**	-0.441**	0.665**	1.000

The hypothesis is confirmed. Imprisonment rates for both crimes are correlated significantly (positively) with population growth and negatively with percent locals.

Criminologists never fully trust a research finding until it has turned up repeatedly. So, had someone created the correlation matrix shown above back in the 1920s (and no one did, partly because social scientists hadn't learned to use correlations at that time), that finding would not still be cited as a major piece of evidence in favor of the social disorganization theory of crime. Social scientists place little confidence in results that have been obtained only once. Instead, confidence in a finding grows to the extent that a hypothesis has been tested again and again on different data and the same result has been obtained. The process of retesting a hypothesis is known as **replication** (it comes from the word *replica*, meaning a copy or reproduction).

In the remainder of this exercise you will have a chance to see if these findings can be replicated in other eras using UCR data on burglary and larceny rates.

Name: *Worksheets* - Exercise 11

> *Workbook exercises and software are copyrighted. Copying is prohibited by law.*

Open the **FIFTYC** data file and select the Correlation function.

1. Use the following variables: **94** or **POP GO 40**, **92** or **BURGLARY40**, and **93** or **LARCENY 40** and fill in the correlation matrix:

	POP GO 40	BURGLARY40	LARCENY 40
POP GO 40			
BURGLARY40			
LARCENY 40			

What is the correlation between burglary and population growth? _____

Is it significant? **(circle one)**   YES   NO

What is the correlation between larceny and population growth? _____

Is it significant? **(circle one)**   YES   NO

Are these correlations stronger or weaker than those for 1923?

               (check one)   ☐ STRONGER THAN 1923   ☐ WEAKER THAN 1923

Do these results replicate those found earlier in this exercise
(is the original hypothesis supported)?   YES   NO

2. Use the following variables: **98** or **NO MOVE 60**, **99** or **POP GO 60**, **96** or **BURGLARY60,** and **97** or **LARCENY 60** and fill in the correlation matrix:

	NO MOVE 60	POP GO 60	BURGLARY60	LARCENY 60
NO MOVE 60				
POP GO 60				
BURGLARY60				
LARCENY 60				

Part IV - *PROPERTY CRIME*   125.

Worksheets - Exercise 11

What is the long label for **NO MOVE 60**? _____

_____

_____

How could this variable be interpreted as a measure of social disorganization?

What is the correlation between burglary and percent who
haven't moved?   _____

Is it significant? (circle one)   YES   NO

What is the correlation between burglary and population growth? _____

Is it significant? (circle one)   YES   NO

Why is one of these correlations negative and the other positive?

What is the correlation between larceny and percent who
haven't moved?   _____

Is it significant? (circle one)   YES   NO

What is the correlation between larceny and population growth? _____

Is it significant? (circle one)   YES   NO

Are these correlations stronger or weaker than those for 1923 and 1940?

(check one) ☐ STRONGER THAN 1923   ☐ WEAKER THAN 1923

(check one) ☐ STRONGER THAN 1940   ☐ WEAKER THAN 1940

Do these results replicate those found earlier in this exercise?   YES   NO

126.   Criminology: *An Introduction Using MicroCase*

Name: _____   **Worksheets** - Exercise 11

3. Use the following variables: **72** or **NEW HOMES**, **100** or **POP GO 80**, **102** or **BURGLARY82,** and **101** or **LARCENY 82** and fill in the correlation matrix:

	NEW HOMES	POP GO 80	BURGLARY82	LARCENY 82
NEW HOMES				
POP GO 80				
BURGLARY82				
LARCENY 82				

What is the long label for **NEW HOMES**? _____

_____

How could this variable be interpreted as a measure of social disorganization?

What is the correlation between burglary and percent new homes? _____

Is it significant? (circle one)   YES   NO

What is the correlation between burglary and population growth? _____

Is it significant? (circle one)   YES   NO

What is the correlation between larceny and percent new homes? _____

Is it significant? (circle one)   YES   NO

What is the correlation between larceny and population growth? _____

Is it significant? (circle one)   YES   NO

Part IV - *PROPERTY CRIME*   127.

Worksheets - Exercise 11

Are the correlations between population growth and burglary and larceny, stronger or weaker than those for 1923 and 1940?

Burglary: (check one) ☐ STRONGER THAN 1923   ☐ WEAKER THAN 1923

(check one) ☐ STRONGER THAN 1940   ☐ WEAKER THAN 1940

Larceny: (check one) ☐ STRONGER THAN 1923   ☐ WEAKER THAN 1923

(check one) ☐ STRONGER THAN 1940   ☐ WEAKER THAN 1940

Do these results replicate those found earlier in this exercise?   YES   NO

4. Use the following variables: **4** or **POP GO 90**, **7** or **P.CRIME**, **12** or **BURGLARY**, and **13** or **LARCENY** and fill in the correlation matrix:

	POP GO 90	P. CRIME	BURGLARY	LARCENY
POP GO 90				
P. CRIME				
BURGLARY				
LARCENY				

What is the correlation between burglary and population growth? _____

Is it significant? (circle one)   YES   NO

What is the correlation between larceny and population growth? _____

Is it significant? (circle one)   YES   NO

What is the correlation between property crimes and population growth? _____

Is it significant? (circle one)   YES   NO

Name: **Worksheets** - Exercise 11

Are the correlations between population growth and burglary and larceny, stronger or weaker than those for 1982?

Burglary: (check one) ☐ STRONGER THAN 1982   ☐ WEAKER THAN 1982

Larceny: (check one) ☐ STRONGER THAN 1982   ☐ WEAKER THAN 1982

Do these results replicate those found earlier in this exercise?   YES   NO

5. Use the variables **41** or **% DIVORCED**, **7** or **P.CRIME**, **12** or **BURGLARY** and **13** or **LARCENY** and fill in the **top row** of the correlation matrix:

	% DIVORCED	P.CRIME	BURGLARY	LARCENY
% DIVORCED				

Are these results relevant to testing the theory of social disorganization? Hint: Could the percent currently divorced be interpreted as a measure of social disorganization? Explain.

Part IV - *PROPERTY CRIME*

EXERCISE 12: High School Offenders

Nearly 4 percent (3.7%) of our national sample of high school seniors reported they had been in "serious trouble with the law." In Exercise 9 we were unable to analyze data on who used cocaine because, although 4.6 of the college sample said they had done so in the past year, that amounted to only 25 people — too few to base an analysis on. But, although an even smaller percentage of this high school sample reported serious trouble with the law, analysis can proceed because in a sample this huge that adds up to 405 students. Now you are going to find who these students are: What distinguishes people who get in trouble with the law from those who don't?

Open the **HISCHOOL** data file and select **B. Tabular Statistics** from the **STATISTICAL ANALYSIS MENU**.

Juvenile delinquents (and most adult offenders, for that matter) seldom specialize. Rather, those who break one law or rule tend to break others.

The hypothesis is: **Students who drink, use marijuana, and cut classes are those most likely to also have been in serious trouble with the law.**

Make **1** or **LAW TROUBL** the row variable, and select **3** or **DRINK/30** as the column variable. When the table appears on the screen *press C for column percentages*.

	NEVER	1 OR 2	3 OR MORE
YES	2.8	2.5	4.6
NO	97.2	97.5	95.4

Students who drank 3 or more times during the past month were almost twice as likely to have been in serious trouble than were students who did not drink that month. *Press S (for Statistics)*. Prob. = 0.000.

Press <ENTER> twice and you will be ready to run a new table.

Make **1** or **LAW TROUBL** the row variable, and select **4** or **MARIJUANA** as the column variable. When the table appears on the screen *press C for column percentages*.

	NEVER	1 OR 2	SOMETIMES	OFTEN
YES	2.1	2.6	2.5	7.4
NO	97.9	97.4	97.5	92.6

Those who used marijuana often that year were more than three times as likely to have been in serious trouble as were those who never used it. *Press S (for Statistics)*. Prob. = 0.000.

Part IV - *PROPERTY CRIME*

Exercise 12

Press <ENTER> twice and you will be ready to run a new table.

Make **1** or **LAW TROUBL** the row variable, and select **2** or **CUT CLASS?** as the column variable. When the table appears on the screen *press C for column percentages*.

	CUTS	DOESN'T
YES	6.0	1.9
NO	94.0	98.1

Those who cut class were more than three times as likely to have been in serious trouble as were those who didn't. *Press S (for Statistics)*. Prob. = 0.000.

Our hypothesis is strongly supported.

Press <ENTER> twice and you will be ready to run a new table.

No variable has as much impact on crime and delinquency as does gender. In any population that has been studied, males are far more likely than females to offend. Consider these data collected and published by INTERPOL in 1992 on the percent female among all persons arrested by the police:

% FEMALE

West Germany	23.5
Japan	20.7
Austria	19.1
United States	18.4
France	17.3
Switzerland	16.7
Canada	14.1
Russia	13.8
Netherlands	10.0
Poland	8.2
England & Wales	4.0
China	2.2

The hypothesis is: **Males will be more likely than females to have been in serious trouble with the law.**

Make **1** or **LAW TROUBL** the row variable, and select **5** or **SEX** as the column variable. When the table appears on the screen *press C for column percentages*.

	MALE	FEMALE
YES	6.5	1.2
NO	93.5	98.8

As expected. Males are more than five times as likely as females to have been in serious trouble. *Press S (for Statistics)*. Prob. = 0.000.

The hypothesis is: Based on our findings for alcohol and drug use, **non-Hispanic whites should be the group MOST likely to have been in serious trouble with the law.**

Make **1** or **LAW TROUBL** the row variable, and select **6** or **RACE/ETH** as the column variable. When the table appears on the screen *press C for column percentages*.

	WHITE	AFRICAN-AM	HISP-AMER	ASIAN-AMER
YES	3.4	2.8	4.3	4.3
NO	96.6	97.2	95.7	95.7

The hypothesis is not supported. Both Hispanic-Americans and Asian-Americans were more apt to report serious trouble with the law, while African-Americans were less likely than non-Hispanic whites to report trouble. *Press S (for Statistics)*. Prob. = 0.023. The results are significant. However, they are not consistent with data on arrest, which show that African-Americans are more likely to be arrested for all categories of offense than are members of other racial and ethnic groups. What might account for this inconsistency?

Discrimination might play a part in who gets arrested, although studies do not suggest that African-American offenders are more likely to be arrested than are offenders in other racial and ethnic groups. However, part of the inconsistency may be an artifact of differential dropout rates. Compared with these other groups, African-Americans are more likely to drop out of school and most dropouts would not have been around to fill out a questionnaire in their senior year. Dropouts are more likely to get in trouble, and hence the lower percentage for African-Americans may be due to the fact that a higher percentage of their "offenders" did not take part in the survey.

Another possibility is that African-American students used a somewhat more stringent standard in deciding what constituted "serious" trouble with the law. For kids in a suburban neighborhood, any contact with the police, even over minor offenses, might be judged as serious. In contrast, kids in a center city neighborhood might disregard any encounter that did not result in a court appearance.

A final factor involves the small numbers of persons in *any* racial or ethnic group who actually commit crimes. That is, while most Americans (and most high school seniors) drink alcohol, very few people commit real crimes — not only have a very small number of these high school seniors gotten in serious trouble, a relatively small number of Americans commit the crimes that constitute our official crime rate. Let's look at some numbers.

Exercise 12

In any recent year, the police have made about 2.3 million arrests of persons accused of committing one or more of the index crimes — the serious crimes reported in the Uniform Crime Report. If no one was arrested twice during the year, then 1.2 percent of Americans would have been arrested in a given year. But, the typical offender is arrested several times a year (when not in jail or prison). Taking repeat offenders into account yields an estimate that about 0.4 percent of Americans get arrested in a given year, or only about 790,000 people out of a population of 200 million (excluding persons under age 16). We also must not assume that the people arrested in a given year are in addition to those arrested in recent prior years. The fact is that the same people tend to get arrested year after year. According to the Bureau of Justice Statistics *Survey of State Prison Inmates, 1991* (March, 1993, NCJ-136949), 81 percent of all persons in state prisons had served a prior term — 20 percent were in prison for at least their sixth term (7 percent had served 11 or more prior terms). While there is no way to calculate the exact percentage of Americans whose behavior produces our crime rates, the number clearly is small relative to the population as a whole — perhaps around 2 million people in all.

Given the small numbers involved, it is quite possible for a group such as African-Americans to be overrepresented among those involved in crime, while only a very small percentage of members of that group are involved.

Even if the data may underestimate the offense rate for African-Americans, they appear to offer a fully valid portrait of who, within any and all racial and ethnic groups, is more likely to have been in trouble.

Now it's time for you to test some hypotheses derived from the major theories of crime and deviance.

Name: _____   **WORKSHEETS** - Exercise 12

Workbook exercises and software are copyrighted. Copying is prohibited by law.

Open the **HISCHOOL** data file and select the Tabular Statistics function.

STRAIN THEORIES of crime and deviance focus on the tension between the desire for rewards and the lack of opportunities to achieve them. Variations in power and privilege are the key elements of strain theories — in effect, if they are to have many things they desire, the poor must turn to crime while the rich and powerful can easily obtain these things by legal means. Whenever people propose that poverty is the "root cause" of crime, they are (knowingly or not) invoking strain theories.

1. The hypothesis is: **Students whose parents have low incomes and little education will be more likely to break the law than will those from privileged backgrounds.**

    Make **1** or **LAW TROUBL** the row variable and **10** or **FAMILY SES** the column variable. *Press C for column percentages.* Fill in the table.

	LOWEST Q	QUARTILE 2	QUARTILE 3	HIGHEST Q
YES	%	%	%	%
NO	%	%	%	%

    V = _____ Prob. = _____

    Is the difference statistically significant? (circle one)   YES   NO

    Is the hypothesis supported or rejected? (circle one)   SUPPORTED   REJECTED

    Make **1** or **LAW TROUBL** the row variable and **8** or **MOM'S ED** the column variable. *Press C for column percentages.* Fill in the table.

	-H.SCHOOL	HI SCHOOL	COLLEGE	POST-GRAD
YES	%	%	%	%
NO	%	%	%	%

    V = _____ Prob. = _____

    Is the difference statistically significant? (circle one)   YES   NO

    Is the hypothesis supported or rejected? (circle one)   SUPPORTED   REJECTED

Part IV - *PROPERTY CRIME*

Worksheets - Exercise 12

Make **1** or **LAW TROUBL** the row variable and **9** or **DAD'S ED** the column variable. *Press C for column percentages.* Fill in the table.

	-H.SCHOOL	HI SCHOOL	COLLEGE	POST-GRAD
YES	%	%	%	%
NO	%	%	%	%

V = _____ Prob. = _____

Is the difference statistically significant? **(circle one)**   YES   NO

Is the hypothesis supported or rejected? **(circle one)**   SUPPORTED   REJECTED

Are these results consistent with results you have obtained in earlier exercises? How would you explain these findings?

CONTROL THEORIES of deviance do not ask why people commit crimes; rather, they ask, Why doesn't everyone? The central idea is that people will break norms unless they find it is in their personal interest not to do so and it is only in their interest to conform when they have more to lose by being caught breaking the law than they could hope to gain from breaking the law. People differ in their stakes in conformity — the things they risk if they deviate — and therefore some people are "free" to break laws because they have little or nothing to lose by it.

Control theories postulate a number of basic kinds of stakes in conformity. **Investments** are the dues we already have paid toward a satisfactory biography and which we expect to sustain a current and/or future flow of rewards. For high school students, a major investment is in school performance. Those who are doing well in school and who look forward to college and a successful career have a lot to lose by getting into serious trouble with the law.

Name: **Worksheets** - Exercise 12

2. The hypothesis is: **Students who are doing well in school and who expect to go to college will be LESS likely to break the law than will those who are not doing well.**

Make **1** or **LAW TROUBL** the row variable and **11** or **GRADES** the column variable. *Press C for column percentages.* Fill in the table.

	A'S OR B'S	WORSE
YES	%	%
NO	%	%

V = _____ Prob. = _____

Is the difference statistically significant? (circle one)   YES   NO

Is the hypothesis supported or rejected? (circle one)   SUPPORTED   REJECTED

Make **1** or **LAW TROUBL** the row variable and **12** or **HOMEWORK** the column variable. *Press C for column percentages.* Fill in the table.

	UNDER 1 HR	1 TO 3 HRS	3 OR MORE
YES	%	%	%
NO	%	%	%

V = _____ Prob. = _____

Is the difference statistically significant? (circle one)   YES   NO

Is the hypothesis supported or rejected? (circle one)   SUPPORTED   REJECTED

Make **1** or **LAW TROUBL** the row variable and **16** or **TO COLLEGE** the column variable. *Press C for column percentages.* Fill in the table.

	NEXT YEAR	MAY LATER	DK/NO
YES	%	%	%
NO	%	%	%

V = _____ Prob. = _____

Is the difference statistically significant? (circle one)   YES   NO

Is the hypothesis supported or rejected? (circle one)   SUPPORTED   REJECTED

Part IV - *PROPERTY CRIME*

Worksheets - Exercise 12

In Exercise 9 you explored another aspect of control theory: **involvements**. The idea here is that the more time and energy one spends in non-deviant activities, the less time and energy one will have for getting into trouble. We saw that the amount of spare time students had, the more apt they were to drink and take drugs.

The hypothesis is: **Students who have time to do a lot of cruising will be MORE likely to break the law than will those who seldom cruise.**

Make **1** or **LAW TROUBL** the row variable and **14** or **CRUISING** the column variable. *Press C for column percentages.* Fill in the table.

	DAILY	1-2 WEEK	NOT OFTEN
YES	%	%	%
NO	%	%	%

V = _____ Prob. = _____

Is the difference statistically significant? (circle one)　　　　　YES　NO

Is the hypothesis supported or rejected? (circle one)　　　SUPPORTED　REJECTED

Make **1** or **LAW TROUBL** the row variable and **15** or **HANGIN'OUT** the column variable. *Press C for column percentages.* Fill in the table.

	DAILY	1-2 WEEK	NOT OFTEN
YES	%	%	%
NO	%	%	%

V = _____ Prob. = _____

Is the difference statistically significant? (circle one)　　　　　YES　NO

Is the hypothesis supported or rejected? (circle one)　　　SUPPORTED　REJECTED

Name: *Worksheets* - Exercise 12

Another element in control theories involves **belief**. The notion here is that what we believe can influence our behavior. Some beliefs encourage commitment to conformity, others justify deviance. An example is this item: *"Good luck is more important than hard work for success."*

The hypothesis is: **Students who think luck will govern their future will be much less concerned about conforming than will those who think success comes from hard work.**

Make **1** or **LAW TROUBL** the row variable and **19** or **LUCK/WORK** the column variable. *Press C for column percentages.* Fill in the table.

	STRONG AGR	AGREE	DISAGREE	STRONG DIS
YES	%	%	%	%
NO	%	%	%	%

V = _____ Prob. = _____

Is the difference statistically significant? **(circle one)**   YES   NO

Is the hypothesis supported or rejected? **(circle one)**   SUPPORTED   REJECTED

Another kind of belief that control theory posits as a basis for conformity are religious beliefs.

The hypothesis is: **The more frequently students attend church, the less apt they are to get in trouble with the law.**

Make **1** or **LAW TROUBL** the row variable and **13** or **CH.ATTEND** the column variable. *Press C for column percentages.* Fill in the table.

	WEEKLY	SOMETIMES	NEVER
YES	%	%	%
NO	%	%	%

V = _____ Prob. = _____

Is the difference statistically significant? **(circle one)**   YES   NO

Is the hypothesis supported or rejected? **(circle one)**   SUPPORTED   REJECTED

Part IV - *PROPERTY CRIME*

Worksheets - Exercise 12

3. Think of yourself as a parent. On the basis of what you have learned thus far, what might you do to try to keep your children out of trouble?

EXERCISE 13: College Offenders

In Exercise 3 we saw that 22 percent of the sample of college students reported that they had been "picked up, or charged, by the police." Students were not asked *when* this took place, but chances are that many of these incidents occurred during high school. Because the question was preceded by one asking about being charged with a traffic offense "other than illegal parking," the students were reporting being in trouble with the police for more serious reasons. The data do not tell us what these reasons were. But, based on an immense wealth of prior research, we can be sure that the overwhelming percentage of these incidents involved property offenses; excluding traffic offenses, about 4 of 5 persons arrested are charged with property crimes.

In this exercise we will try to see what kinds of students were more likely to have been picked up by the police.

The hypothesis is: **People who break one law are apt to break others. College students who have been picked up by the police will also be more likely to report they have shoplifted.**

Open the **COLLEGEC** data file and select **B. Tabular Statistics**. Now the screen asks you for the name or number of the row variable. *Type* **2** or **PICKED UP?** and *press <ENTER>*. Make **3** or **SHOPLIFT?** the column variable. When the screen asks for a control variable, simply *press <ENTER>*. When the screen asks for a subset variable, simply *press <ENTER>*. When this table appears on the screen *press C for column percentages*.

	YES	NO
PICKED UP	33.6	11.7
NOT	66.4	88.3

The hypothesis is strongly supported. Students who have shoplifted are about three times as likely to also report having been picked up. *Press S (for Statistics)*. Prob. = 0.000.

Press <ENTER> twice and you will be ready to run a new table.

The hypothesis is: **Following the same logic, we can predict that students who get traffic tickets will be more likely to have been picked up by the police for non-traffic offenses.**

Select **2** or **PICKED UP?** as the row variable and **1** or **TICKET?** as the column variable. *Press C for column percentage*.

Part IV - *PROPERTY CRIME*

Exercise 13

	YES	NO
PICKED UP	29.8	12.9
NOT	70.2	87.1

The hypothesis is strongly supported. Students who have received traffic tickets are nearly three times as likely to also report having been picked up. *Press S (for Statistics)*. Prob. = 0.000.

Press <ENTER> twice and you will be ready to run a new table.

The hypothesis is: **We also can predict that students who have drunk alcohol in the past year will be more likely to get picked up.**

Make **2** or **PICKED UP?** the row variable, and select **4** or **DRINK?** as the column variable. When the table appears on the screen *press C for column percentages*.

	DRINK NOW	ABSTAIN NO
PICKED UP	25.4	14.9
NO	74.6	85.1

This hypothesis also is strongly supported. *Press S (for Statistics)*. Prob. = 0.006. While only about 15 percent of those who have not drunk alcohol in the past year say they have been picked up, 25.4 percent of those who did drink say they have been picked up by the police. Keep in mind that, although they may also have been picked up for drunk driving, that is not the offense involved in variable 2.

Press <ENTER> twice and you will be ready to run a new table.

The hypothesis is: **We also can predict that students who use marijuana will be more likely to get picked up.**

Make **2** or **PICKED UP?** the row variable, and select **6** or **POT NOW** as the column variable. When the table appears on the screen *press C for column percentages*.

	PAST YEAR	NO
YES	39.7	13.2
NO	60.3	86.8

The hypothesis is strongly supported. Nearly 40 percent of students who have used marijuana in the past year have been picked up, compared with 13.2 percent of non-users. *Press S (for Statistics)*. Prob. = 0.000.

Press <ENTER> twice and you will be ready to run a new table.

Despite the small number of cocaine users in this sample, so few categories are involved in either variable that a comparison is possible (barely).

The hypothesis is: **We also can predict that students who used cocaine during the past year will be more likely to get picked up**.

Make **2** or **PICKED UP?** the row variable, and select **7** or **COKE NOW** as the column variable. When the table appears on the screen *press C for column percentages*.

	PAST YEAR	NOT
PICKED UP	64.0	20.0
NO	36.0	80.0

Cocaine use identifies a highly "crime-prone" subgroup within this college population. Nearly two-thirds of users say they have been picked up by the police. *Press S (for Statistics)*. Prob. = 0.000.

Press <ENTER> twice and you will be ready to run a new table.

The hypothesis is: **Males will be more apt than females to have been picked up.**

Make **2** or **PICKED UP?** the row variable, and select **10** or **SEX** as the column variable. When the table appears on the screen *press C for column percentages*.

	FEMALE	MALE
PICKED UP	15.4	29.3
NOT	84.6	70.7

The hypothesis is strongly supported. Male students are nearly twice as likely as females to report having been picked up. *Press S (for Statistics)*. Prob. = 0.000. Notice, however, that this gender difference among college students is far smaller than among high school students, as seen in Exercise 8.

Press <ENTER> twice and you will be ready to run a new table.

The hypothesis is: Based on findings about drinking and drug use, **students who belong to fraternities or sororities will be more likely than other students to have been picked up by the police**.

Make **2** or **PICKED UP?** the row variable, and select **9** or **WHERE LIVE** as the column variable. When the table appears on the screen *press C for column percentages*.

Part IV - *PROPERTY CRIME*

Exercise 13

	WITH PAREN	OWN APARTM	DORM	SORORITY	FRATERNITY
PICKED UP	17.0	25.3	13.3	15.7	46.0
NOT	83.0	74.7	86.7	84.3	54.0

Clearly, our hypothesis is incorrect as to sororities, but it is supported for fraternities — whose members are far more likely than students living elsewhere to have been picked up. *Press S (for Statistics).* Prob. = 0.000. However, this result should be checked among males since they are more apt to have been picked up and all fraternity residents are male.

Make **2** or **PICKED UP?** the row variable, and select **9** or **WHERE LIVE** as the column variable. *Press <ENTER>* to skip the control variable option. When the screen asks for a subset variable, use **10** or **SEX** and make **2** as the lower limit and then use **2** as the upper limit. This will limit the table to males. When the table appears on the screen *press C for column percentages*.

	WITH PAREN	OWN APARTM	DORM	FRATERNITY
PICKED UP	23.9	29.6	15.0	46.0
NOT	76.1	70.4	85.0	54.0

The differences are reduced substantially, but males living in fraternities still are significantly more likely to have been picked up. *Press S (for Statistics).* Prob. = 0.002.

Your turn.

| Name: | **WORKSHEETS** - Exercise 13 |

Workbook exercises and software are copyrighted. Copying is prohibited by law.

Open the **COLLEGEC** data file and select the Tabular Statistics function.

1. The hypothesis is: **Non-Hispanic white students will be more likely to have been picked up by the police than Asian-American students.**

    Make **2** or **PICKED UP?** the row variable and **11** or **WH/ASIAN** the column variable. *Press C for column percentages.* Fill in the table.

	WHITE	ASIAN
PICKED UP	%	%
NOT	%	%

    V = _____ Prob. = _____

    Is the difference statistically significant? **(circle one)**   YES   NO

    Is the hypothesis supported or rejected? **(circle one)**   SUPPORTED   REJECTED

2. The hypothesis is: Based on previous results: **Students from upper-income families will be no less likely than students from low-income families to have been picked up by the police.**

    Make **2** or **PICKED UP?** the row variable and **12** or **FAMILY $** the column variable. *Press C for column percentages.* Fill in the table.

	BELOW AV.	AVERAGE	ABOVE AV.	FAR ABOVE
PICKED UP	%	%	%	%
NOT	%	%	%	%

    V = _____ Prob. = _____

    Is the difference statistically significant? **(circle one)**   YES   NO

    Is the hypothesis supported or rejected? **(circle one)**   SUPPORTED   REJECTED

3. The hypothesis is: **Students who smoke will be more likely to have been picked up by the police than those who do not.**

Part IV - *PROPERTY CRIME*

Worksheets - Exercise 13

Make **2** or **PICKED UP?** the row variable and **19** or **SMOKE?** the column variable. *Press C for column percentages. Fill in the table.*

	NON-SMOKER	SMOKER
PICKED UP	%	%
NOT	%	%

V = _____ Prob. = _____

Is the difference statistically significant? (circle one)   YES   NO

Is the hypothesis supported or rejected? (circle one)   SUPPORTED   REJECTED

Check this finding for each gender.

Make **2** or **PICKED UP?** the row variable and **19** or **SMOKE?** the column variable and **10** or **SEX** the control variable. *Press C for column percentages. Fill in the table.*

FEMALES

	NON-SMOKER	SMOKER
PICKED UP	%	%
NOT	%	%

V = _____ Prob. = _____

Is the difference statistically significant? (circle one)   YES   NO

Is the hypothesis supported or rejected? (circle one)   SUPPORTED   REJECTED

Press <ENTER> twice to see the next table. Press C for column percentages. Fill in the table.

MALES

	NON-SMOKER	SMOKER
PICKED UP	%	%
NOT	%	%

V = _____ Prob. = _____

Is the difference statistically significant? (circle one)   YES   NO

Is the hypothesis supported or rejected? (circle one)   SUPPORTED   REJECTED

Name: *Worksheets* - Exercise 13

How would you explain these results?

4. The hypothesis is: **Students who have had several sex partners will be more likely to have been picked up by the police than those who have had none or only one sex partner.**

   Make **2** or **PICKED UP?** the row variable and **18** or **SEX PARTNR** the column variable. *Press C for column percentages.* Fill in the table.

	NONE	ONE	2-3	4 OR MORE
PICKED UP	%	%	%	%
NOT	%	%	%	%

   V = _____ Prob. = _____

   Is the difference statistically significant? (circle one)   YES NO

   Is the hypothesis supported or rejected? (circle one)   SUPPORTED REJECTED

   Check this finding for each gender.

   Make **2** or **PICKED UP?** the row variable and **18** or **SEX PARTNR** the column variable and **10** or **SEX** the control variable. *Press C for column percentages.* Fill in the table.

Part IV - *PROPERTY CRIME*   147.

Worksheets - Exercise 13

FEMALES

	NONE	ONE	2-3	4 OR MORE
PICKED UP	%	%	%	%
NOT	%	%	%	%

V = _____ Prob. = _____

Is the difference statistically significant? **(circle one)** YES NO

Is the hypothesis supported or rejected? **(circle one)** SUPPORTED REJECTED

Press <ENTER> twice to see the next table. Press C for column percentages. Fill in the table.

MALES

	NONE	ONE	2-3	4 OR MORE
PICKED UP	%	%	%	%
NOT	%	%	%	%

V = _____ Prob. = _____

Is the difference statistically significant? **(circle one)** YES NO

Is the hypothesis supported or rejected? **(circle one)** SUPPORTED REJECTED

Comparing the values of V, is the correlation larger among males or among females? **(circle one)** MALES FEMALES

Suggest reasons why the relationship between the number of sexual partners and being picked up might be a bit different for women than for men.

148. Criminology: *An Introduction Using MicroCase*

PART V: *VIOLENT CRIME*

Crimes of violence make up only 12 percent of all of the index crimes included in the *Uniform Crime Report*. But, when people express their concerns about crime, it usually is violent crime they have in mind, for these are the crimes we all fear.

In the three exercises that follow you will explore various aspects of violent crime.

EXERCISE 14: Analyzing Violent Crime Rates

The violent crime rate — which combines the rates for murder, rape, robbery, and assault — has been rising rapidly during the past decade. From 1981 through 1990, violent crimes per 100,000 population increased by 33.7 percent. The increases were not uniform across violent crime categories, however. Murder increased by 4.1 percent while aggravated assault increased by 58.9 percent. In fact, because assaults make up nearly 60 percent of all violent crimes, the huge increase in this rate accounts for most of the overall increase. This alone raises questions about the value of an overall rate of violent crimes. To begin this exercise, let's pursue that question in greater detail.

Open the **FIFTYC** data file and select **E. Mapping Variables** from the **STATISTICAL ANALYSIS MENU**. Now the screen asks you for the name or number of the variable you wish to map. *Type* **8** or **HOMICIDE** and *press* <ENTER>.

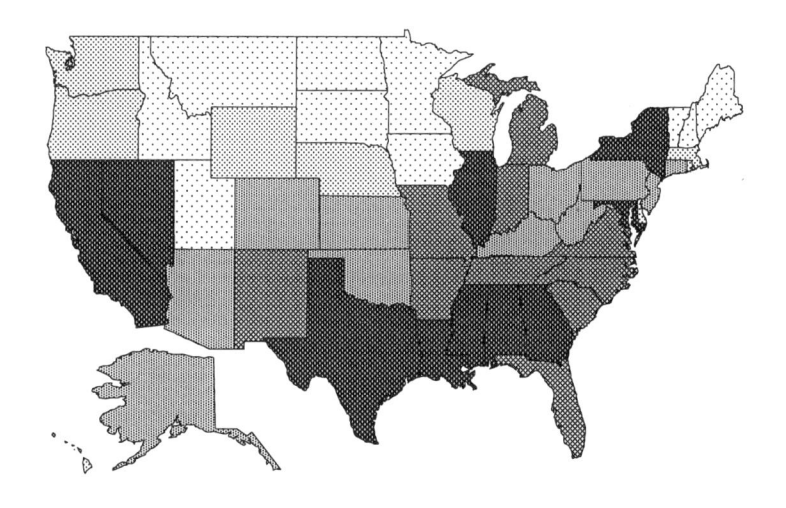

1992: Homicides per 100,000

Notice that homicide tends to be highest across the southern portion of the nation, a belt stretching from the Carolinas around to California (plus New York and Maryland). *Type N (for Name)* to see which state had the highest rate. Louisiana was highest with a rate of 17.4 per 100,000 in population. *Press the down arrow to see the next highest state*. New York was second with a rate of 13.2. *Press D (for Distribution)* and all 50 states will appear on the

Part V - *VIOLENT CRIME* 149.

Exercise 14

screen, ranked from high to low. South Dakota was lowest with 0.6, followed by New Hampshire and Iowa, tied at 1.6.

Press <ENTER> twice to clear the screen and you will be ready to create another map. Map **9** or **RAPE**.

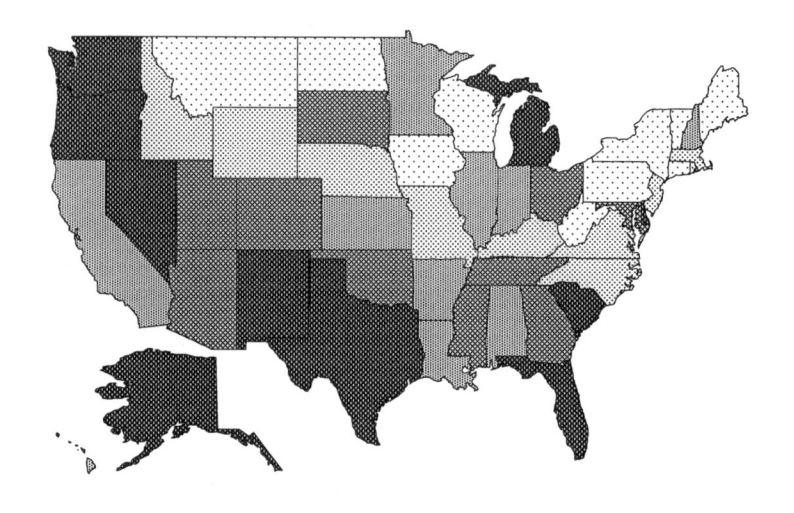

1992: Rapes per 100,000

This map isn't like the homicide map. In fact, there is no clear geographic pattern to the rape rate — the highest states are scattered across the major regions. *Type N (for Name)* to see which state had the highest rate. Alaska was highest with a rate of 99 per 100,000 population. *Press the down arrow to see the next highest state.* Delaware was second with a rate of 86. *Press D (for Distribution)* and all 50 states will appear on the screen, ranked from high to low. Michigan was third, Washington was fourth, New Mexico and Nevada tied for fifth. Iowa was lowest with 19, followed by West Virginia with 22.

Press <ENTER> twice to clear the screen and you will be ready to create another map. Map **10** or **ROBBERY**.

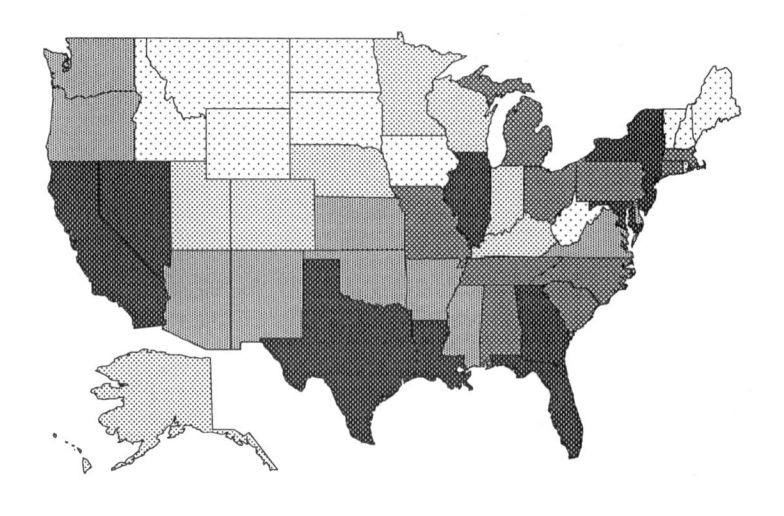

1992: Robberies per 100,000

Exercise 14

The robbery map is more like the homicide map. However, it seems to be more urban than homicide. *Type N (for Name)* to see which state had the highest rate. New York was highest with a rate of 597 per 100,000 in population. *Press the down arrow to see the next highest state.* Maryland was second with a rate of 429. *Press D (for Distribution)* and all 50 states will appear on the screen, ranked from high to low. California was third, Illinois was fourth, Florida was fifth, followed by Nevada. North Dakota was lowest with 8, followed by Vermont with 9.

Press <ENTER> twice to clear the screen and you will be ready to create another map. Map **11** or **ASSAULT**.

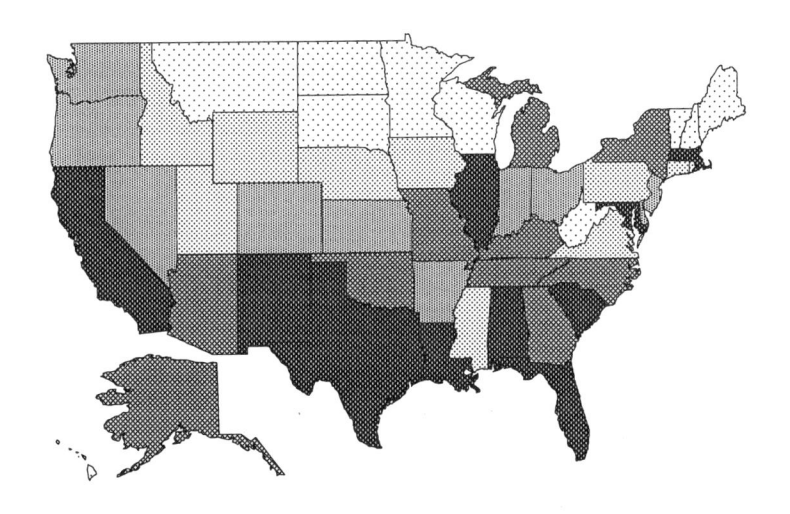

1992: Assaults per 100,000

The assault map is much like the homicide map — there is something of the same "wrap-around" of the southern part of the nation. *Type N (for Name)* to see which state had the highest rate. Florida was highest with a rate of 777 per 100,000 in population. *Press the down arrow to see the next highest state.* New Mexico was second with a rate of 724. *Press D (for Distribution)* and all 50 states will appear on the screen, ranked from high to low. South Carolina was third, Alabama was fourth, Louisiana was fifth, followed by California. As usual, North Dakota was lowest with 50.

By comparing these maps we can see that the geography of various violent crimes tends to differ. Another way to see this is through correlations.

Select **G. Correlation**. Use the four violent crime variables (variables 8 through 11) and this screen will appear:

Part V - *VIOLENT CRIME*

Exercise 14

	HOMICIDE	RAPE	ROBBERY	ASSAULT
HOMICIDE	1.000	0.251*	0.731**	0.722**
RAPE	0.251*	1.000	0.159	0.410**
ROBBERY	0.731**	0.159	1.000	0.623**
ASSAULT	0.722**	0.410**	0.623**	1.000

The first important thing to notice here is that rape is not highly correlated with the other three violent crimes. In fact, the correlation between rape and robbery is not significant. On the other hand, homicide and assault are very highly correlated (0.722), as they should be. After all, many homicides were intended only as assaults and some assaults were attempts at murder. Finally, although robbery is highly correlated with homicide and assault, the correlation is low enough to permit different relationships with other variables. To see this, repeat the above correlation matrix, but add **26** or **% METROPOL** as the first variable. Give your attention to the first column of the table, as shown below:

	% METROPOL
% METROPOL	1.000
HOMICIDE	0.360**
RAPE	0.153
ROBBERY	0.709**
ASSAULT	0.414**

Clearly, robbery is very urban — highly correlated with the percent of a state's population resident in metropolitan areas. Homicide is far less urban (0.360), and rape is not significantly related to urbanism. Assault is more urban than homicide and rape, but much less so than robbery.

These findings suggest that research should not be based on a combined measure of violent crime. Each should be analyzed separately.

Your turn.

Name: **Worksheets** - Exercise 14

Workbook exercises and software are copyrighted. Copying is prohibited by law.

1. In 1990, a total of 9,724 whites and 9,744 blacks in the United States were murder victims — separate statistics are not published for Hispanics or Asians. Translated into rates, 4.6 whites per 100,000 were murdered and 31.6 blacks per 100,000 were murdered. That suggests the following hypothesis: **Homicide rates will be strongly, positively correlated with the percent of the population that is black.**

    Open the **FIFTYC** data file and select the scatterplot function. Create the following scatterplot:

    Dependent variable: **8** or **HOMICIDE**
    Independent variable: **19** or **%AFRICAN-A**

What is the correlation coefficient?	r = _____
Is this a positive or negative correlation? (circle one)	POSITIVE NEGATIVE
Is the difference statistically significant? (circle one)	YES NO
Is the hypothesis supported or rejected? (circle one)	SUPPORTED REJECTED

2. In 1990, 78 percent of all murder victims were male. That suggests the following hypothesis: **Homicide rates will be strongly, positively, correlated with the proportion of male households.**

    Create the following scatterplot:

    Dependent variable: **8** or **HOMICIDE**
    Independent variable: **44** or **MALE HOMES**

What is the correlation coefficient?	r = _____
Is this a positive or negative correlation? (circle one)	POSITIVE NEGATIVE
Is the difference statistically significant? (circle one)	YES NO
Is the hypothesis supported or rejected? (circle one)	SUPPORTED REJECTED

Part V - *VIOLENT CRIME*

Worksheets - Exercise 14

3. As defined by the UCR, rape is limited to female victims. That suggests the following hypothesis: **Rape rates will be higher where a larger proportion of the population is made up of single, adult females and males**.

   Select the Correlation function and use **9** or **RAPE**, **46** or **%SINGLEMEN**, and **47** or **%SINGL FEM** and fill in the correlation matrix.

	RAPE	%SINGLEMEN	%SINGLE FEM
RAPE			
%SINGLE MEN			
%SINGLE FEM			

   What is the correlation between rape and single males? _____

   Is it significant? (circle one)   YES   NO

   What is the correlation between rape and single females? _____

   Is it significant? (circle one)   YES   NO

   Is the hypothesis supported or rejected? (circle one)   SUPPORTED   REJECTED

   Were you surprised by this particular outcome? Explain.

4. Let's try a variant on our hypothesis: **Rape rates will be higher where a larger proportion of the population is made up of divorced adults and female-headed households**.

154.   Criminology: *An Introduction Using MicroCase*

Name: _____ **Worksheets** - Exercise 14

Use **9** or **RAPE**, **41** or **% DIVORCED**, and **43** or **% FEMHEAD** and fill in the correlation matrix.

	RAPE	% DIVORCED	% FEMHEAD
RAPE			
% DIVORCED			
% FEMHEAD			

What is the correlation between rape and percent divorced? _____

Is it significant? (circle one)   YES   NO

What is the correlation between rape and female-headed households? _____

Is it significant? (circle one)   YES   NO

Is the hypothesis supported or rejected? (circle one)   SUPPORTED   REJECTED

Can you suggest reasons why these variables are correlated with rape, while the single population is not?

5. Much has been written about the connection between drugs and violent crime. That suggests this hypothesis: **Higher rates of cocaine addiction will be positively correlated with violent crime rates.**

   Use **65** or **COKE USERS**, **8** or **HOMICIDE**, **10** or **ROBBERY**, and **11** or **ASSAULT** and fill in the first column of the correlation matrix.

Part V - *VIOLENT CRIME*   155.

Worksheets - Exercise 14

	COKE USERS
COKE USERS	
HOMICIDE	
ROBBERY	
ASSAULT	

What is the correlation between coke users and homicide? _____

Is it significant? (circle one)   YES   NO

What is the correlation between coke users and robbery? _____

Is it significant? (circle one)   YES   NO

What is the correlation between coke users and assault? _____

Is it significant? (circle one)   YES   NO

Is the hypothesis supported or rejected? (circle one)   SUPPORTED   REJECTED

Which correlation is strongest? _____

Can you suggest why cocaine addiction has more impact on this rate than on the others?

6. Since no discussion of crime on TV ever seems to end without mention of high school dropout rates, the hypothesis is: **Higher rates of dropping out of school will be positively correlated with violent crime rates**.

Use **49** or **% DROPOUTS**, **8** or **HOMICIDE**, **10** or **ROBBERY**, and **11** or **ASSAULT** and fill in the first column of the correlation matrix.

Name: **Worksheets** - Exercise 14

	% DROPOUTS
% DROPOUTS	
HOMICIDE	
ROBBERY	
ASSAULT	

What is the correlation between dropouts and homicide? _____

Is it significant? **(circle one)** YES NO

What is the correlation between dropouts and robbery? _____

Is it significant? **(circle one)** YES NO

What is the correlation between dropouts and assault? _____

Is it significant? **(circle one)** YES NO

Is the hypothesis supported or rejected? **(circle one)** SUPPORTED REJECTED

Part V - *VIOLENT CRIME*

EXERCISE 15: Whose Friends Are Getting Murdered?

Open the **NORC** data file and go to **A. Univariate Statistics** on the **STATISTICAL ANALYSIS MENU**. Select **4** or **KNOW MURD.** as the variable. After the pie chart appears *type D*.

Within the past 12 months, how many people have you known personally that were victims of homicide?

	Frequency	%
NONE	1244	90.8
ONE	81	5.9
2 OR MORE	45	3.3

Altogether, one American in ten claims to have known someone murdered in the past year. In this exercise you are going to find out who these people are — whose friends are getting killed?

Switch to **B. Tabular Statistics**. About three of four murder victims are male. So the hypothesis is: **Men are more likely than women to know a murder victim.**

Make **4** or **KNOW MURD.** the row variable, and select **21** or **SEX** as the column variable when the table appears. *Press C for column percentages*.

	MALE	FEMALE
NONE	89.7	91.7
ONE	6.1	5.7
2 OR MORE	4.2	2.6

The hypothesis is completely rejected. Men and women are equally likely to know murder victims. *Press S (for Statistics)*. Prob.= 0.258. Upon reflection, this makes sense. Men are more likely to become murder victims, but most people are known to about the same number of males and females.

Press <ENTER> twice and you will be ready to run another table.

In recent years, more than 60 percent of murder victims were under the age of 35. This suggests the hypothesis that **Younger people will be more apt to have known a murder victim.**

Make **4** or **KNOW MURD.** the row variable, and select **25** or **AGE** as the column variable when the table appears. *Press C for column percentages*.

Part V - *VIOLENT CRIME*

Exercise 15

	18-29	30-39	40-49	50-65	OVER 65
NONE	87.7	88.4	90.2	91.4	97.3
ONE	7.6	7.1	6.7	5.3	2.3
2 OR MORE	4.7	4.5	3.1	3.3	0.4

The hypothesis is confirmed. People under 30 are more likely to know murder victims. *Press S (for Statistics)*. Prob. = 0.011.

Press <ENTER> twice and you will be ready to run another table.

About two-thirds of all murder victims are killed by gunshot wounds. This suggests the hypothesis that **People who own guns will be more apt to have known a murder victim.**

Make **4** or **KNOW MURD.** the row variable, and select **15** or **OWN GUN?** as the column variable. *Press C for column percentages.*

	HAS GUN	NO GUN
NONE	93.3	89.6
ONE	4.4	6.7
2 OR MORE	2.3	3.7

The hypothesis is rejected. *Press S (for Statistics)*. Prob. = 0.156.

Press <ENTER> twice and you will be ready to run another table.

Nearly 90 percent of all murders occur in major metropolitan areas. This suggests the hypothesis that **People who live in large cities will be more apt to have known a murder victim.**

Make **4** or **KNOW MURD.** the row variable, and select **19** or **PLACE SIZE** as the column variable. *Press C for column percentages.*

	CITY	SUBURB	TOWN	RURAL
NONE	86.1	92.9	91.4	91.4
ONE	8.6	5.2	4.6	4.9
2 OR MORE	5.3	1.8	4.1	3.8

Criminology: *An Introduction Using MicroCase*

The hypothesis is confirmed. People in large cities are more likely to know murder victims. *Press S (for Statistics)*. Prob. = 0.015.

Press <ENTER> twice and you will be ready to run another table.

In a substantial number of homicides, both the victim and the perpetrator were intoxicated. This suggests the hypothesis that **People who frequently go to bars or taverns will be more apt to have known a murder victim than will people who do not go out drinking**.

Make **4** or **KNOW MURD.** the row variable, and select **11** or **GO TO BARS** as the column variable. *Press C for column percentages*.

	WEEKLY	SOMETIMES	NEVER
NONE	86.3	89.8	90.0
ONE	5.0	6.9	6.9
2 OR MORE	8.8	3.3	3.1

The hypothesis is rejected. *Press S (for Statistics)*. Prob. = 0.158.

Press <ENTER> twice and you will be ready to run another table.

Our hypothesis is: **People who get drunk will be more likely to know murder victims than will people who don't get drunk or who abstain from alcohol use.**

Make **4** or **KNOW MURD.** the row variable, and select **13** or **DRUNK** as the column variable. *Press C for column percentages*.

	GETS DRUNK	NO	ABSTAINS
NONE	89.5	92.6	91.3
ONE	5.5	4.7	6.5
2 OR MORE	5.0	2.7	2.3

Absolutely nothing! *Press S (for Statistics)*. Prob. = 0.370.

Press <ENTER> twice and you will be ready to run another table.

The hypothesis is: **Upper-income people are far less likely to become murder victims and therefore ought to be less likely to know them.**

Make **4** or **KNOW MURD.** the row variable, and select **26** or **FAMILY $** as the column variable. *Press C for column percentages*.

Exercise 15

	UNDER $12K	$12K-$23K	$23K-$35K	$35-$60K	OVER $60K
NONE	88.0	90.8	92.2	90.2	90.7
ONE	5.8	6.8	5.4	7.6	6.4
2 OR MORE	6.2	2.4	2.3	2.2	2.9

Not significant. *Press S (for Statistics)*. Prob. = 0.197.

Your turn.

Name: _____   **Worksheets** - Exercise 15

> *Workbook exercises and software are copyrighted. Copying is prohibited by law.*

1. Has anyone you knew personally ever been a murder victim? **(circle one)** YES   NO

    IF YES: please describe this person (age, sex, race, etc.) and say how you happened to know him or her.

2. What might it do to someone to have been personally acquainted with a murder victim? Perhaps it would make that person more favorable toward capital punishment? Stated as a hypothesis: **People who know a murder victim will be more apt to favor execution of murderers.**

    Open the **NORC** data file and select the Tabular Statistics function. In this instance we will make **7** or **EXECUTE?** the row variable and select **4** or **KNOW MURD.** as the column variable. *Press C for column percentages.* Fill in the table.

	NONE	ONE	2 OR MORE
FAVOR	%	%	%
OPPOSE	%	%	%

    Is the difference statistically significant? **(circle one)**   YES   NO

    Is the hypothesis supported or rejected? **(circle one)**   SUPPORTED   REJECTED

    Does this result surprise you? Explain.

Part V - *VIOLENT CRIME*   163.

Worksheets - Exercise 15

3. Another plausible hypothesis is: **People who know a murder victim will be more apt to fear walking around in their neighborhood at night.**

   Make **1** or **FEAR WALK** the row variable, and select **4** or **KNOW MURD.** as the column variable. *Press C for column percentages.* Fill in the table.

	NONE	ONE	2 OR MORE
YES	%	%	%
NO	%	%	%

   Prob. = _____

   Is the difference statistically significant? (circle one)   YES   NO

   Is the hypothesis supported or rejected? (circle one)   SUPPORTED   REJECTED

   Does this result surprise you? Explain.

4. Perhaps this will work: **People who know a murder victim will be more apt to favor gun control laws.**

   Make **14** or **GUN LAW?** the row variable, and select **4** or **KNOW MURD.** as the column variable. *Press C for column percentages.* Fill in the table.

	NONE	ONE	2 OR MORE
FAVOR	%	%	%
OPPOSE	%	%	%

   Prob. = _____

Name: _____ ***Worksheets*** - Exercise 15

    Is the difference statistically significant? **(circle one)**   YES   NO

    Is the hypothesis supported or rejected? **(circle one)**   SUPPORTED   REJECTED

Does this result surprise you? Explain.

5. The hypothesis is: **Crime rates are correlated — high in some places, low in others. Therefore, people who have been burglarized in the past year are more likely to know someone who has been murdered.**

   Make **4** or **KNOW MURD.** the row variable, and select **2** or **BURGLED?** as the column variable. *Press C for column percentages.* Fill in the table.

	YES	NO
NONE	%	%
ONE	%	%
2 OR MORE	%	%

       Prob. = _____

       Is the difference statistically significant? **(circle one)**   YES   NO

       Is the hypothesis supported or rejected? **(circle one)**   SUPPORTED   REJECTED

   Does this result surprise you? Explain.

Part V - *VIOLENT CRIME*

Worksheets - Exercise 15

6. As was noted in Exercise 14, African-Americans are far more likely than others to become murder victims. That suggests the following hypothesis ought to hold: **African-Americans are more likely than whites to know someone who became a murder victim.**

   Make **4** or **KNOW MURD.** the row variable, and select **23** or **W/AF-A** as the column variable. *Press C for column percentages.* Fill in the table.

	WHITE	AFRICAN-AM
NONE	%	%
ONE	%	%
2 OR MORE	%	%

   Prob.= _____

   Is the difference statistically significant? **(circle one)**   YES   NO

   Is the hypothesis supported or rejected? **(circle one)**   SUPPORTED   REJECTED

   Does this result surprise you? Explain.

PART VI: *MULTI-VARIATE ANALYSIS*

In several previous exercises you have worked with control variables. That is called multi-variate analysis — any analysis involving more than two variables at a time. In these last two exercises, which are meant to be optional (depending on what your instructor wishes to cover), you will discover a simple method for examining the joint effects of several independent variables on a dependent variable. Then you will discover an especially valuable reason for doing multi-variate analysis.

EXERCISE 16: Violence and the Old West: Regression

In this exercise we will pursue the question: **Was the Old West really violent?**

Those of us who have seen a lot of western movies may find the question silly. But, in recent years some social historians have in fact suggested that the "Wild West" was a myth created by dime novelists and sustained by Hollywood. Indeed, such revisionism has even found its way into the popular press. Recently, *The New York Times* solemnly reported that the scale of homicides in modern America dwarfs that of the Old West: "In its busiest year, the Boot Hill cemetery in rough-and-tumble Dodge City, Kansas, welcomed only 20 gunfighters." In contrast, 2,245 persons were murdered in New York City in 1990.

Exercise 1 should have alerted you to the dangers of using raw numbers to make comparisons. Thus, before agreeing with the *Times* editorialist that 20 dead gunfighters is a very small number, we will want to calculate a rate. Since Dodge City never had a population larger than 3,000, 20 dead gunfighters in one year would by themselves have constituted a homicide rate of 667 per 100,000, which is almost 25 times higher than the rate for New York City in 1990 (26.9 per 100,000), and hundreds of times higher than the rates for Philadelphia, Boston, and New York in this same era. Moreover, presumably some gunfighters who were shot down in Dodge City that year left funds sufficient to avoid entombment in Boot Hill and thus were omitted from this count. Nor does this total include any ordinary, non-gunfighting citizens who may have been murdered that year. All-in-all, it's hard to imagine a place with a homicide rate as high as it must have been in Dodge City. In comparison, modern American cities seem relatively peaceful, as these 1990 homicide rates per 100,000 suggest:

New Orleans	31.2
New York	26.9
Houston	21.1
Los Angeles	19.9
Miami	19.9
Detroit	16.3
Atlanta	13.7
Philadelphia	13.2
San Francisco	9.2
San Diego	8.6
Phoenix	8.2

Exercise 16

Now that you have been alerted to the need to use rates, not raw numbers, for comparisons, let us return to our question: Just how violent was the western frontier in the 19th century? To get started, the first thing we will have to do is find a way of identifying, or locating, the frontier.

Open the **FIFTYC** data file and select **E. Mapping Variables**. *Type* **82** or **OLD WEST18** and *press <ENTER>*. The map that appears identifies the frontier areas in 1860 as simply a function of how far west they are. (A number of states remain blank because they were not yet states in 1860, and West Virginia remains blank because it was not created as a separate state from Virginia until after the Civil War.)

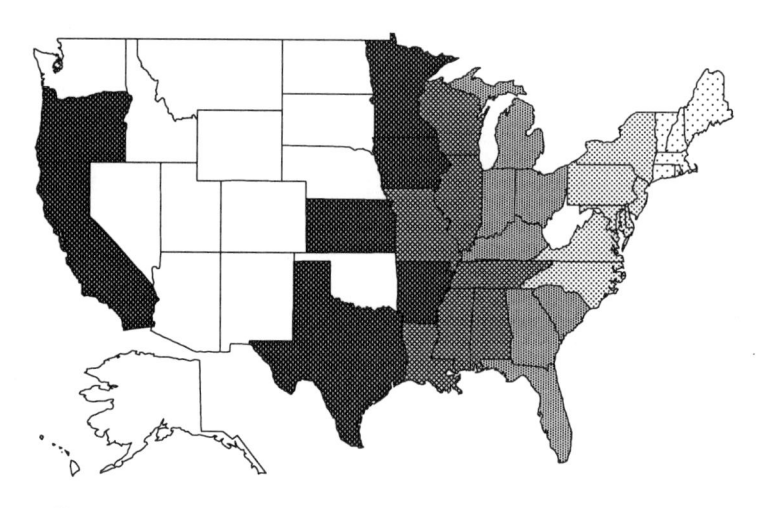

Degrees on longitude west of prime meridian of state capital

Type N (for Name). In 1860, on the eve of the Civil War, Oregon was the most westerly state, followed by California and Texas.

Now map **83** or **NEWNESS 18**. *Type N (for Name)*. This variable is based on the date when a state was admitted to the union, minus 1787 — the year the first states entered the union. Thus Pennsylvania scored zero on newness, being among the oldest states, while Kansas scored 74 as the newest state.

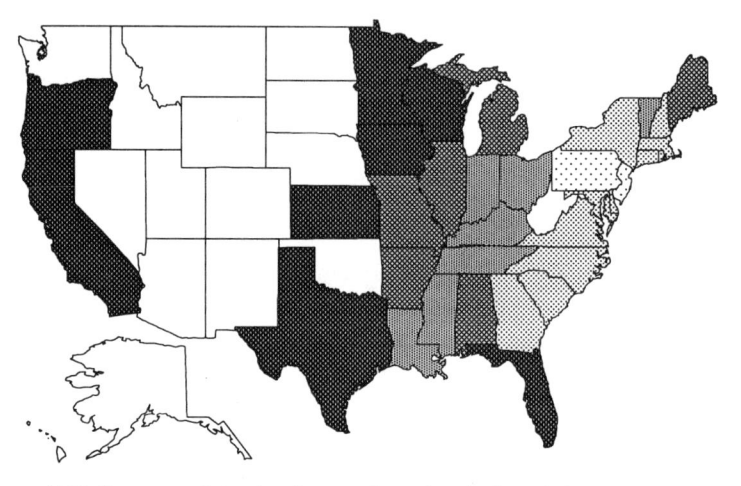

1860: Newness of statehood: year of statehood minus 1787

Exercise 16

Frontiers also typically are boom areas where rapid population growth is taking place. So map **81** or **POP GO1860**. This map will appear.

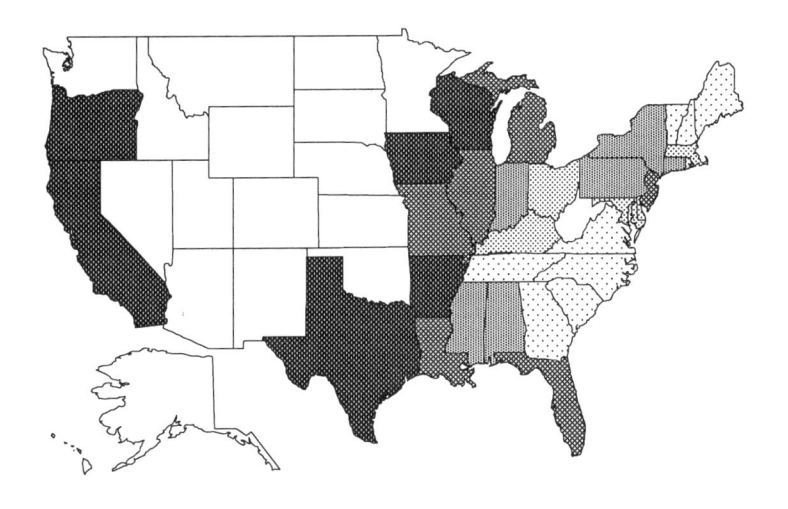

1850-60: Percent population growth (–decline)

This map shows the percentage rate of population growth between 1850 and 1860. Clearly, the fastest growing states were western. *Type N (for Name)*. California grew fastest between 1850 and 1860 — 310.4 percent. Oregon was close behind. *Press D (for Distribution)*. Vermont hardly grew at all — 0.3 percent — and New Hampshire wasn't growing much faster.

Now that we have found the frontier in 1860, let's see how violent it was. Map **79** or **HOMICIDE18**. This map will appear:

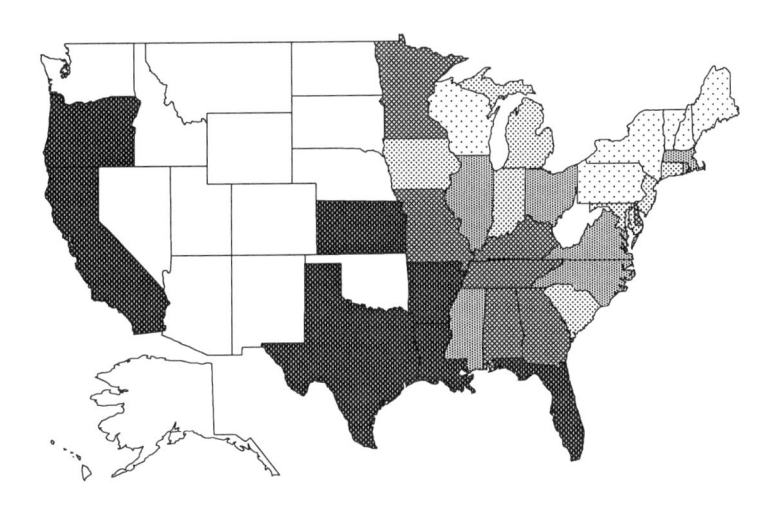

1860: Homicides per 100,000

Type N (for Name) to see which state is highest — Texas, with a rate of 20.03 homicides per 100,000 population. California is second with 19.74. In contrast, in 1860 many states had homicide rates of less than 1 per 100,000. It is clear that in terms of

Part VI - *MULTI-VARIATE ANALYSIS*

Exercise 16

homicide rates, the frontier areas were far more violent than the rest of the nation. However, before we compare these rates with those for 1990, it is important to know how these figures were collected.

In this era the federal government did not receive crime statistics from local law enforcement agencies, nor did it receive data on causes of death from local coroners' reports. Beginning in 1850, the census-takers asked at each household whether anyone in the household had died in the past year, and if so, what was the cause of death. Eventually it was demonstrated that mortality statistics gained in this way greatly underreported the number of deaths and were subject to errors as to cause because survivors sometimes were mistaken. Moreover, many survivors didn't truly know what had been the cause of death — often the attending physician, when there was one, didn't know either.

Of course, such problems are minimized for violent deaths. Nevertheless, state rates of deaths due to homicide based on census interviews are no doubt *far lower* than the true rates, if for no other reason than victims who left no surviving household had no one to report their deaths to the census-takers. Presumably, homicide victims would have been over-selected from among the ranks of single, male drifters who populate the saloon scenes in cowboy movies. Therefore, underreporting of homicides would have been greatest on the frontiers, where men like this tended to congregate.

Keeping in mind that the 1860 data undoubtedly underestimate homicide rates, let's compare these results with those for 1993. Map **8** or **HOMICIDE**. This map will appear.

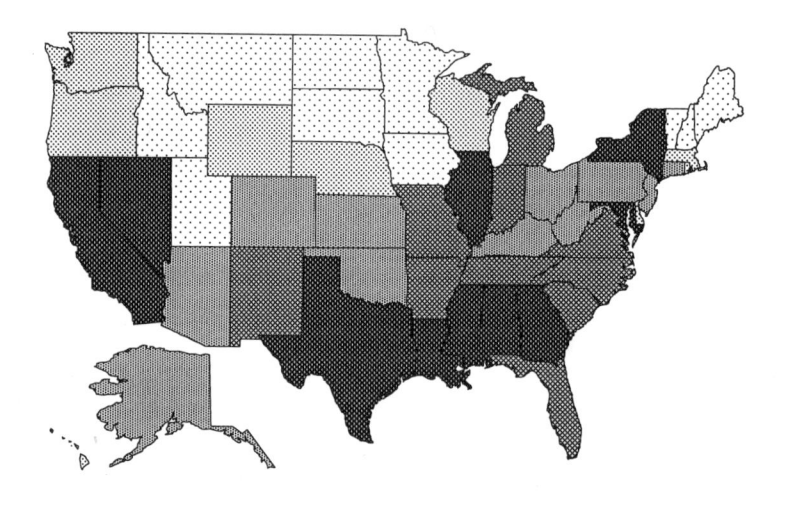

1992: Homicides per 100,000

This map shows official homicide rates for 1990. *Type N (for Name)*. Louisiana was highest with 17.4 homicides per 100,000, New York was second with 13.2. *Press D (for Distribution)*. Texas was third. As was true in 1860, New Hampshire had a very low rate. Comparing the two maps we find that the states with the highest homicide rates in 1860 had higher rates than the highest states in 1990, but the differences aren't huge. Does that mean that the Old West wasn't so wild after all? No. For one thing, the modern rates are far more complete — very few homicides go unreported to the police and their reports to the F.B.I. are carefully checked. A second factor has to do with what people in the Wild West were willing to call murder.

Exercise 16

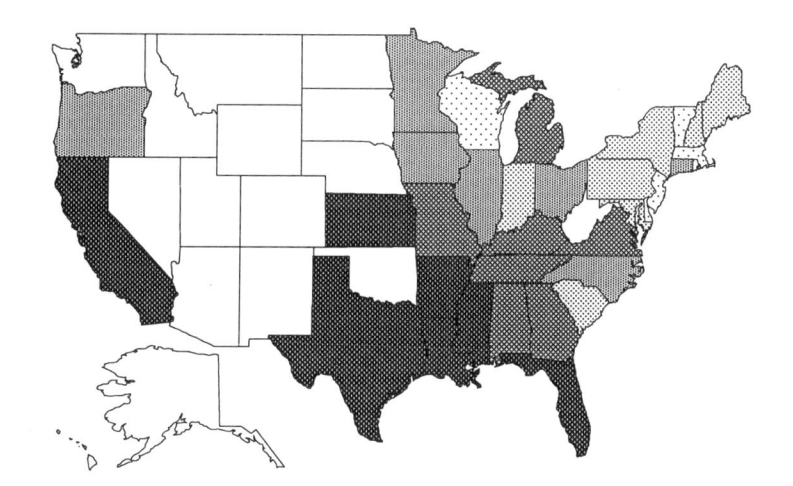

Map **78** or **GUN KILL 18**. This map will appear.

1860: Deaths from accidental gunshot wounds per 100,000

In addition to learning of deaths caused by homicide, the census-takers recorded the number of deaths from "accidental" gunshot wounds. If the data adequately reflect underlying social reality, then the two ought to be very highly correlated on the grounds that where there are lots of guns, lots of people get murdered and lots of others get shot unintentionally — in fact, along the frontiers a lot of people probably got shot accidentally on purpose. *Type N (for Name)*. California was highest with 11.32 accidental gunshot deaths per 100,000. Texas was next highest with 8.44. *Press D (for Distribution)*. Kansas was third and Louisiana was fourth. In contrast, the rates were very low in the Northeast. If we were to assume that most of these deaths were not really accidents, and add the rates together, then the homicide rates for the Old West would be very high indeed: California's rate would be 31.1 and Texas' rate would be 28.2 — or double the 1990 rates.

As noted, these two rates should be very highly correlated. Switch to **G. Correlation**. Make **79** or **HOMICIDE18** the first variable and **78** or **GUN KILL18** the second. You will find that the two are extremely highly correlated (r = .858).

Now, let's test the hypothesis: **In 1860, homicide rates were highest on the western frontier**. Correlate these variables: **79** or **HOMICIDE18**, **82** or **OLD WEST18**, **83** or **NEWNESS 18**, and **81** or **POP GO1860**.

	HOMICIDE18	OLD WEST18	NEWNESS 18	POP GO1860
HOMICIDE 18	1.000	0.769**	0.599**	0.694**
OLD WEST18	0.769**	1.000	0.757**	0.861**
NEWNESS 18	0.599**	0.757**	1.000	0.821**
POP GO1860	0.694**	0.861**	0.821**	1.000

Part VI - *MULTI-VARIATE ANALYSIS*

Exercise 16

These all are high correlations, supporting the hypothesis.

Exercise 4 noted that correlation does not necessarily demonstrate causation — variables may be highly correlated without one being the cause of the other. It would seem silly to suggest, for example, that the correlation between **POP GO1860** and **NEWNESS 18** reflects cause-and-effect. States aren't newer because their population is growing faster, nor are they growing faster because they are newer.

However, the hypothesis we just tested does imply causation (as have most of the hypotheses we have tested thus far in the course). That is, we aren't interested in "accidental" correlations between measures of the Old West and homicide. Instead, we think that social and cultural conditions typical of the Old West *caused* high homicide rates. That we found the predicted correlations does not prove a cause-and-effect relationship exists. But, had we failed to find these correlations, we could have been sure that no causal relationship existed.

Thus far we have used correlations to tell us the degree to which two variables are related to one another. For example, we can see above that population growth is highly correlated with the homicide rate — that where the population grew more rapidly, the homicide rates were higher. But what if we wanted to see the effect of two independent variables on a third variable — the **combined effects** of population growth and of westernness on homicide, for example? We know that each of these variables is highly correlated with homicide and with one another. To sort out these correlations, social scientists use a technique called **multiple regression**.

Switch to **I. Regression**. The screen asks for the name or number of the dependent variable. In this instance the variable we wish to explain, the one we think of as being caused, is homicide. So, type **79** or **HOMICIDE18** and *press <ENTER>*. The screen asks for the name or number of the first independent variable. Type **81** or **POP GO1860** and *press <ENTER>*. The screen asks for the name or number of the second independent variable. Type **82** or **OLD WEST18** and *press <ENTER>*. When the screen asks for the name or number of the third independent variable, type nothing, simply *press <ENTER>*. Do not select a subset. This graphic will appear on the screen:

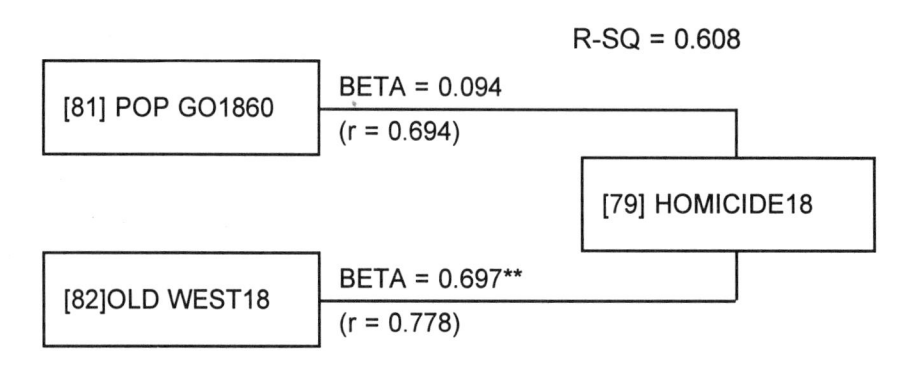

R-SQ = 0.608

[81] POP GO1860 — BETA = 0.094 (r = 0.694) — [79] HOMICIDE18

[82] OLD WEST18 — BETA = 0.697** (r = 0.778) — [79] HOMICIDE18

In the upper right-hand corner, the screen reads: R-SQ = 0.608. This stands for R^2, which is **a measure of the combined effects** of the two independent variables on the dependent variable. In plain English, this means that variables 81 and 82 together account for 61 percent of the variation in homicide rates across the states in 1860. Put another way, if all states had grown by the same percentage from 1850 to 1860 and if all of them had been equally western, there would have been 61 percent less variation in their homicide rates.

But, that's not all we can see in this graphic. Beneath each of the horizontal lines is the value of r, which is Pearson's correlation coefficient. These are, of course, the same as those shown in the set of correlations we already have examined. Above each line is the word **BETA**, followed by a numerical value. This stands for the standardized beta, which estimates **the independent effect of each independent variable on the dependent variable**.

Because both of the independent variables in this analysis are very highly correlated, to a considerable extent they overlap and measure the same thing — in this case the location of the frontier. What regression does is to sort out the independent contributions of these two variables. And what we discover is that population growth influences homicide rates *only* because it is highly correlated with geography — growth tended to be high in the West. But, with the effects of the West removed, growth is not correlated with variations in homicide. We know this because the BETA for population growth is tiny (0.09) and not statistically significant (no asterisks follow the value of BETA). On the other hand, the BETA for Old West is a huge 0.70, and the two asterisks indicate it is statistically significant above the 0.01 level.

Let's try another. *Press <ENTER>* to clear the screen. This time use **79** or **HOMICIDE18** as the dependent variable and *press <ENTER>*. The screen asks for the name or number of the first independent variable. Type **83** or **NEWNESS 18** and *press <ENTER>*. The screen asks for the name or number of the second independent variable. Type **82** or **OLD WEST18** and *press <ENTER>*. When the screen asks for the name or number of the third independent variable, type nothing, simply *press <ENTER>*. Do not select a subset. This graphic will appear on the screen:

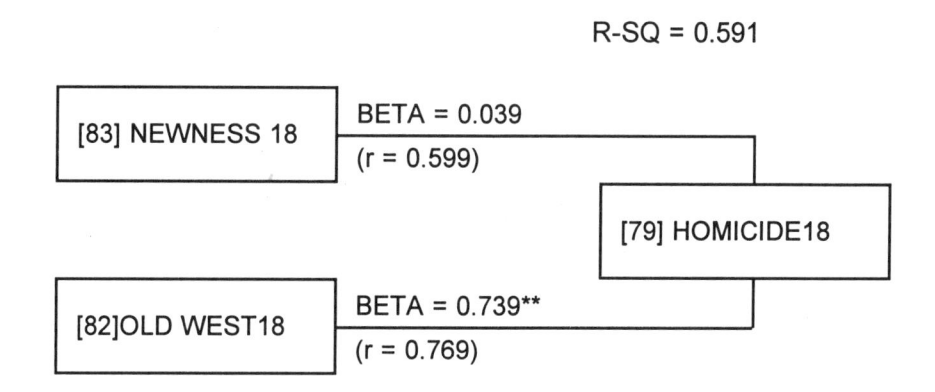

R-SQ = 0.591

```
[83] NEWNESS 18    BETA = 0.039
                   (r = 0.599)
                                    [79] HOMICIDE18
[82] OLD WEST18    BETA = 0.739**
                   (r = 0.769)
```

Again we find that the whole effect is caused by the **OLD WEST18** variable. It has a BETA of 0.74, significant above the 0.01 level. **NEWNESS 18** has no independent effect (BETA = 0.04) and is not significant.

Now, let's see what happens if we use all three of these independent variables at one time. Use **79** or **HOMICIDE18** as the dependent variable and *press <ENTER>*. The screen asks for the name or number of the first independent variable. Type **81** or **POP GO1860** and *press <ENTER>*. The screen asks for the name or number of the second independent variable. Type **82** or **OLD WEST18** and *press <ENTER>*. When the screen asks for the

Part VI - *MULTI-VARIATE ANALYSIS*

Exercise 16

name or number of the third independent variable, type **83** or **NEWNESS 18** and *press <ENTER>*. When the screen asks for the name or number of the fourth independent variable, type nothing, simply *press <ENTER>*. Do not select a subset. This graphic will appear on the screen:

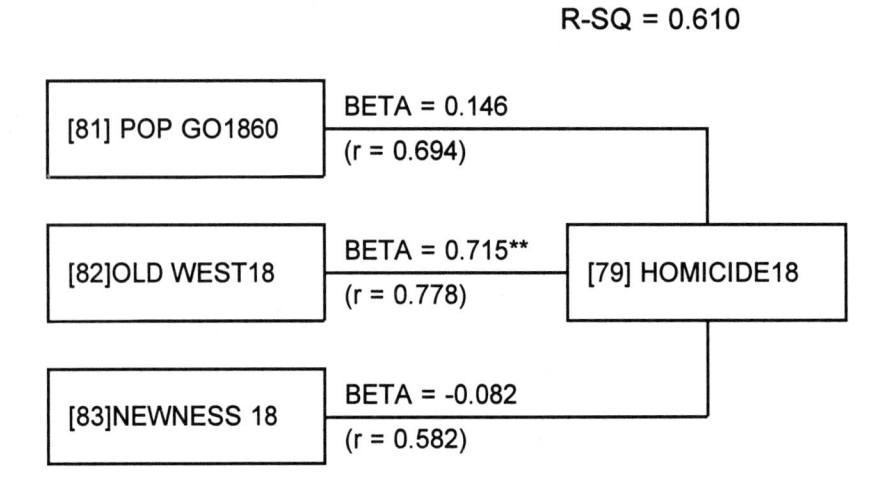

R-SQ = 0.610

```
[81] POP GO1860 ──── BETA = 0.146 ────┐
                    (r = 0.694)        │
                                       │
[82] OLD WEST18 ──── BETA = 0.715** ── [79] HOMICIDE18
                    (r = 0.778)        │
                                       │
[83] NEWNESS 18 ──── BETA = -0.082 ────┘
                    (r = 0.582)
```

These results confirm those found in the three variable analyses — Old West accounts for all of the effect, the BETAS for the other two are insignificant.

So, now we know that homicide rates were highly related to geography in 1860. And you know how to do regression analysis in order to discover the **joint,** or **combined, effects** of several independent variables and their **individual,** or **net, effects**.

Now, you can discover *why* the West was so violent.

Name: _____   **_Worksheets_** - Exercise 16

> *Workbook exercises and software are copyrighted. Copying is prohibited by law.*

1. *Open* the **FIFTYC** data file and select the mapping function. Use the F3 key to open the codebook window and place the highlight on **85** or **S.RATIO 18**. Now press the right arrow key in order to see the long label for this variable.

    Write in the long label: _____
    _____
    _____

    Now map this variable.

    List the three highest states: 1 _____

    2 _____

    3 _____

    List the three lowest states: 32 _____

    33 _____

    34 _____

    Does this map resemble the map of homicide for 1860? **(circle one)**   YES   NO

2. Repeat the above procedure for variable **86** or **HERDS PC18**.

    Write in the long label: _____
    _____
    _____

    Now map this variable.

    List the three highest states: 1 _____

    2 _____

    3 _____

Part VI - *MULTI-VARIATE ANALYSIS*   175.

Worksheets - Exercise 16

    List the three lowest states: 31 _____

                                                                    32 _____

                                                                    33 _____

    Does this map resemble the map of homicide? **(circle one)**   YES   NO

3. Repeat the above procedure for variable **84** or **CHURCHED18**.

    Write in the long label: _____

    _____

    _____

Now map this variable.

    List the three highest states: 1 _____

                                                           2 _____

                                                           3 _____

    List the three lowest states: 32 _____

                                                          33 _____

                                                          34 _____

    Does this map resemble the map of homicide? **(circle one)**   YES   NO

4. Repeat the above procedure for variable **87** or **%BLACK1860**.

    Write in the long label: _____

    _____

    _____

Now map this variable.

    List the three highest states: 1 _____

                                                           2 _____

                                                           3 _____

Name: _____   **Worksheets** - Exercise 16

List the three lowest states: 32 _____

33 _____

34 _____

Does this map resemble the map of homicide? (circle one)   YES   NO

5. Use the correlation function and fill in the following correlations:

	OLD WEST18	S.RATIO 18	HERDS PC18
OLD WEST18			
S.RATIO 18			
HERDS PC18			

6. The hypothesis is: **Where there are an excess of men and a lot of livestock, homicide rates will be high.**

Use the regression function to fill in this diagram:

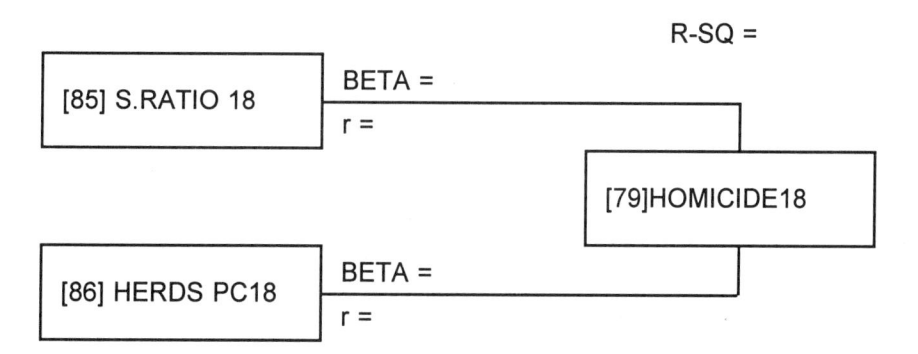

R-SQ =

[85] S.RATIO 18 — BETA = / r = → [79] HOMICIDE18

[86] HERDS PC18 — BETA = / r = → [79] HOMICIDE18

What is the combined effect of these two independent variables? _____

What is the independent or net effect of **S.RATIO 18**? _____

Significant? (circle one)   YES   NO

What is the independent or net effect of **HERDS PC18**? _____

Significant? (circle one)   YES   NO

Is the hypothesis supported or rejected? (circle one)   SUPPORTED   REJECTED

Part VI - *MULTI-VARIATE ANALYSIS*

Worksheets - Exercise 16

7. The hypothesis is: **When included in a regression with an excess of men and of livestock, the Old West will not have an independent effect on homicide.**

   Fill in this regression diagram:

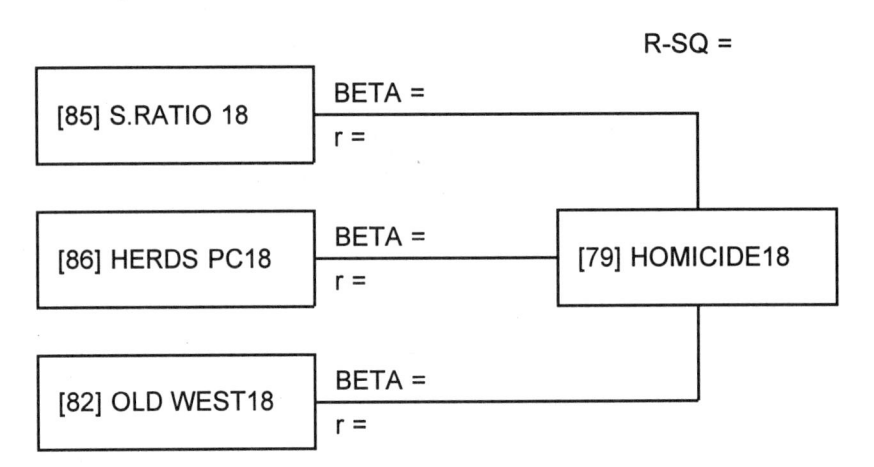

   R-SQ =

   [85] S.RATIO 18 — BETA = , r = → [79] HOMICIDE18

   [86] HERDS PC18 — BETA = , r = → [79] HOMICIDE18

   [82] OLD WEST18 — BETA = , r = → [79] HOMICIDE18

   What is the combined effect of these three independent variables? _____

   What is the independent or net effect of **S.RATIO 18**? _____

   Significant? (circle one)   YES   NO

   What is the independent or net effect of **HERDS PC18**? _____

   Significant? (circle one)   YES   NO

   What is the independent or net effect of **OLD WEST18**? _____

   Significant? (circle one)   YES   NO

   Is the hypothesis supported or rejected? (circle one)   SUPPORTED   REJECTED

On the basis of your research, were the movies correct about why the Old West was violent? Explain.

Read On

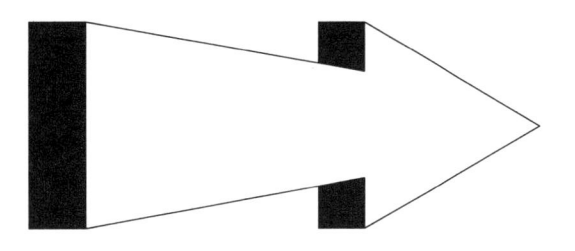

The Daily Tribune

"In Vino Veritas"

©MCMLCII, Tres Gatos Publications   97¢

Military Training Turns People into Gun Freaks

By P.C. Tooter

Military veterans develop a lifelong fascination with firearms, according to a new study released yesterday.

The research, based on a national sample of American adults, found that persons who have served in the armed forces are far more likely than other Americans to own guns, to hunt, and to oppose gun control legislation.

According to Dr. Fred Butz, director of the study, a deep dependency on firearms is instilled during basic training. "Recruits are seduced into a kind of love affair with their weapons."

"Then, if they get to use their weapons and kill people, they develop a lifelong need to cause death that drives them into the forests and fields every hunting season," Butz said.

"Veterans who did not use their weapons to kill people turn to hunting to compensate for having been denied the chance to kill."

Butz is a criminologist at Backwater State University. He began his study three years ago with a $1 million grant from the Zorro Foundation.

When contacted for comments on this study, the famous Dr. Royce Sisters agreed that the connections between military trainees and their firearms are deeply sexual in origin. "In my clinical experience I invariably have found that military veterans regard their weapons in a sexual way. They don't realize that, of course. It is buried too deeply in their subconscious. And masochism plays a role here too."

Asked for comments, Buck Hammer, national commander of the Veterans of Foreign Wars, said, "Either these idiots don't understand guns or sex — maybe neither."

Hunting Reduces Murder

APE--Contrary to the popular belief that hunting makes people indifferent to bloodshed, a new study has found that hunting seems to make people less likely to commit murder.

States where a larger percentage of the population goes hunting, have lower homicide rates.

"Apparently hunting lets people vent their rage on animals, thus saving the lives of human beings," according to the study's author, Dr. Patty Potts.

Dr. Potts is on the faculty of Silo Tech in Gackle, N. D., well-known as the "buckle of the wheat belt."

EXERCISE 17: "Mass Media" Criminology: Detecting Spuriousness

In recent years the news media have begun to report a lot of social science research. Some of the stories are accurate and some of the research is well-done. But, it often seems that the more poorly done the research, or the more obviously silly the conclusions drawn from it, the more likely it is to be selected for press coverage.

In this last exercise you will discover how good researchers try to guard against foolish research findings. And the best way to begin is with the two stories from the fake newspaper on the previous page.

Open the **NORC** data file and select Tabular Statistics. Use **15** or **OWN GUN?** as the row variable and use **17** or **VETERAN?** as the column variable. When the table appears *press C for column percents*. This is what you will see:

	NOT VET	VETERAN
HAS GUN	37.8	57.0
NO GUN	62.2	43.0

It looks like Dr. Fred Butz is right. Veterans are more likely than non-veterans to own guns. *Press S (for Statistics)*. The table is highly significant (Prob. = 0.000).

Next use **16** or **HUNT?** as the row variable and use **17** or **VETERAN?** as the column variable. When the table appears *press C for column percents*. This is what you will see:

	NOT VET	VETERAN
HUNTS	19.5	26.2
NOT HUNTS	80.5	73.8

This table also agrees with Dr. Fred Butz's claims. Veterans are more likely than non-veterans to hunt. *Press S (for Statistics)*. The table is highly significant (Prob. = 0.020).

Next use **14** or **GUN LAW?** as the row variable and use **17** or **VETERAN?** as the column variable. When the table appears *press C for column percents*. This is what you will see:

Part VI - *MULTI-VARIATE ANALYSIS*

Exercise 17

	NOT VET	VETERAN
FAVOR	84.3	71.6
OPPOSE	15.7	28.4

Once again the results agree with Dr. Fred Butz. Veterans are more likely than non-veterans to oppose gun control laws. *Press S (for Statistics)*. The table is highly significant (Prob. = 0.000).

It is not surprising that these results agree with Dr. Butz because there is no reason to doubt his claim to have based his findings on a properly conducted national survey. Therefore, our data should produce the same results his did. What is at issue here is the question of cause. Is the military experience the true cause of these differences?

In earlier exercises you have often noted correlations that seemed unlikely to represent cause-and-effect. Now, it is time to see that many correlations may seem to reflect cause-and-effect, but do not. These are known as **spurious correlations** or relationships. Before doing more with Dr. Butz's findings, let's examine a very obvious instance of spuriousness.

Not long ago an actual research study was reported in the national press that showed that men over age 70 who married women under age 40 lived longer than other men their age. The media seemed convinced by the researcher's claim that this showed that a young wife extended an older man's life expectancy. That is, marrying a younger women *caused* these men to live longer. However, if you stop and think about this claim for a moment (which the researcher seems not to have done), you'll probably figure out that older men who marry young women will tend to be healthier than those who do not — men in nursing homes are unlikely to marry *anyone*, let alone a younger woman. Hence, the correlation between having a young wife and living longer was spurious — both factors were caused by something else, good health.

There is a simple way to detect spurious relationships. In the instance above, the researcher should have compared men who were equally healthy and would have discovered no life expectancy difference between those who took younger wives and those who did not. That is, when health is not allowed to vary, then the relationship between marrying young women and life expectancy should vanish. Let's explore this method further by going back to Dr. Butz and his claims about veterans.

Clearly, Dr. Butz is right that veterans do differ from non-veterans in terms of guns and hunting. But do veterans differ from non-veterans in **another** way or ways that could cause these correlations? What about this?

Use **21** or **SEX** as the row variable and use **17** or **VETERAN?** as the column variable. When the table appears *press C for column percents*. This is what you will see:

	NOT VET	VETERAN
MALE	33.0	96.2
FEMALE	67.0	3.8

Nearly all veterans are men. Two-thirds of non-veterans are women. Is it possible that what we have been seeing are gender differences, not differences attributable to military service? There is an easy way to find out.

Use **15** or **OWN GUN?** as the row variable and use **17** or **VETERAN?** as the column variable and use **21** or **SEX** as the control variable. When the table appears *press C for column percents*. This table is limited to men.

	NOT VET	VETERAN
HAS GUN	49.4	57.3
NO GUN	50.6	42.7

Here the differences between veterans and non-veterans are much smaller than when both males and females were included. *Press S (for Statistics)*. The table is not significant (Prob. = 0.055). *Press <ENTER> twice* and the table for women will appear. There is nothing to see because there are too few female veterans to compare with non-veterans.

What about hunting? Use **16** or **HUNT?** as the row variable and use **17** or **VETERAN?** as the column variable and use **21** or **SEX** as the control variable. When the table appears *press C for column percents*. This table is limited to men.

	NOT VET	VETERAN
HUNTS	31.9	26.6
NOT HUNTS	68.1	73.4

Here the differences between veterans and non-veterans are essentially zero. *Press S (for Statistics)*. The table is not significant (Prob. = 0.162). *Press <ENTER> twice* and the table for women will appear. Again there is nothing to see because there are too few female veterans to compare with non-veterans.

What about gun control? Use **14** or **GUN LAW?** as the row variable and use **17** or **VETERAN?** as the column variable and use **21** or **SEX** as the control variable. When the table appears *press C for column percents*. This table is limited to men.

Exercise 17

	NOT VET	VETERAN
FAVOR	76.0	71.1
OPPOSE	24.0	28.9

Here again the differences between veterans and non-veterans are essentially zero. *Press S (for Statistics)*. The table is not significant (Prob. = 0.168). *Press <ENTER> twice* and the table for women will appear.

When **MALE** veterans and non-veterans are compared, there are no significant differences between them in terms of owning guns, hunting, or support for gun control legislation. Dr. Butz got people excited over nothing. It would have to be a very dead news day for the mass media to be interested in his actual finding that men are more into guns and hunting than are women.

Now, what about the story that hunting reduces murder rates? *Open* the **FIFTYC** data file and go to the **F. Scatterplot** function. Make **8** or **HOMICIDE** the dependent variable and **61** or **HUNTING** the independent variable. When the screen appears you will see that there is a strong negative correlation (−0.466) just as Professor Potts claimed. And it is highly significant, Prob. = 0.000.

Switch to the mapping function and map **8** or **HOMICIDE**. Notice that it is very heavily concentrated in the Sun Belt states. Now map **61** or **HUNTING**. It is very concentrated in the states of the northern Great Plains and in the Rocky Mountains. In Idaho, the Dakotas, and Montana more than half the population buys a hunting license. Now map this variable: **73** or **WARM WINTR**. This is the average January low temperature, the higher a state's average low, the warmer its winters. Not surprisingly the Sun Belt states are warmest and the northern Great Plains states are lowest (North Dakota is -3). Notice too how much this map looks like the homicide map. In effect, the coldest states have the lowest homicide rates.

The fact is that, nationally, homicide fluctuates with the seasons. The highest rates are always in July and August, the lowest rates are in January and February. Homicide is an interaction crime, unlike burglary (burglars do their best to avoid contact with their victims). Factors that limit interaction, reduce homicide. Cold weather reduces interaction and thus reduces homicides. This is supported by two additional facts. First, homicide does not vary by season in the states with very warm winters. Second, nationally homicide rates always show a second, sudden peak in December — when so many holiday gatherings occur and greatly increase interaction. Finally, hunting is highest in the coldest states because that's where the hunting is best. Now let's use regression to see if cold weather eliminates the correlation between hunting and homicide.

Select the regression task and enter **8** or **HOMICIDE** as the dependent variable and **61** or **HUNTING** and **73** or **WARM WINTR** as the independent variables. The following graphic will result:

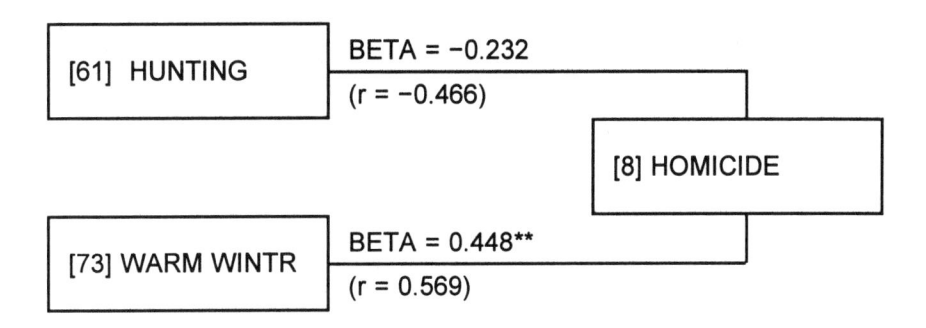

```
[61] HUNTING   BETA = -0.232
               (r = -0.466) ─────────┐
                                     │
                              [8] HOMICIDE
                                     │
[73] WARM WINTR  BETA = 0.448** ─────┘
                 (r = 0.569)
```

And it does. The beta between hunting and homicide has fallen to non-significance. Professor Potts's correlation is spurious.

The **principle for detecting spurious relations** is that when other relevant factors are controlled, a spurious relationship *disappears*. With sex controlled, veterans were not "gun freaks" compared with non-veterans. With weather controlled, states with high rates of hunting do not have lower rates of homicide.

Your turn.

Name: **Worksheets** - Exercise 17

Workbook exercises and software are copyrighted. Copying is prohibited by law.

Open the **FIFTYC** data file and select the Correlation function.

1. **The News in Brief**: *Playboy* causes divorce, experts say.

    Use **56** or **PLAYBOY**, **40** or **DIVORCE**, and **41** or **% DIVORCED** and fill in the correlation matrix:

	PLAYBOY	DIVORCE	%DIVORCED
PLAYBOY			
DIVORCE			
%DIVORCED			

    What is the correlation between the Playboy circulation rate and the divorce rate? _____

    Is it significant? (circle one)　　　　　　　　　　　　　　　　YES　NO

    What is the correlation between the Playboy circulation rate and the percent of the population currently divorced? _____

    Is it significant? (circle one)　　　　　　　　　　　　　　　　YES　NO

    Go to the regression function and fill in the following regression diagram.

    R-SQ =

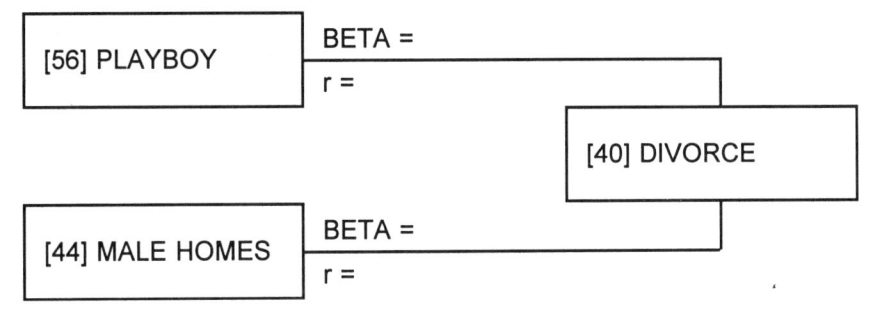

    [56] PLAYBOY — BETA = / r =

    [40] DIVORCE

    [44] MALE HOMES — BETA = / r =

    What is the combined effect of these two independent variables? _____

    What is the independent or net effect of Playboy? _____

Part VI - *MULTI-VARIATE ANALYSIS*

Worksheets - Exercise 17

Significant? (circle one)   YES   NO

What is the independent or net effect of male homes? _____

Significant? (circle one)   YES   NO

Would you challenge the news report in light of this regression analysis? Explain.

Now, fill in this regression diagram:

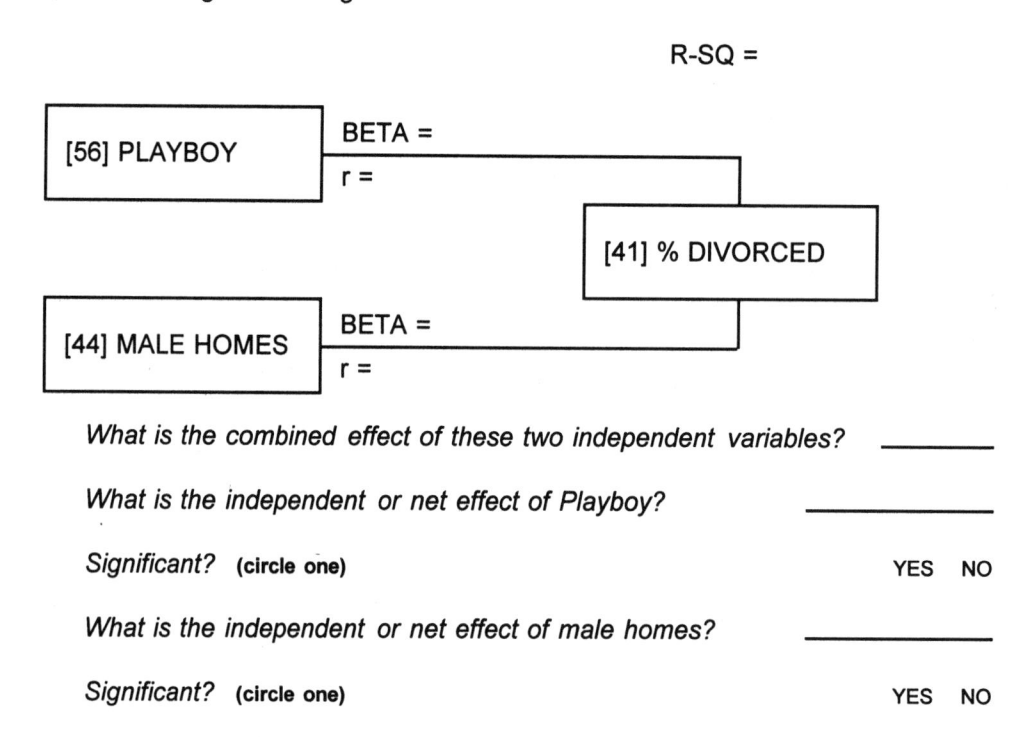

R-SQ =

```
[56] PLAYBOY ──BETA =──┐
             ──r =─────┤
                       ├──[41] % DIVORCED
[44] MALE HOMES ──BETA =┤
                ──r =───┘
```

What is the combined effect of these two independent variables? _____

What is the independent or net effect of Playboy? _____

Significant? (circle one)   YES   NO

What is the independent or net effect of male homes? _____

Significant? (circle one)   YES   NO

Name: Worksheets - Exercise 17

Would you challenge the news report in light of this regression analysis? Explain.

2. **The News in Brief:** *Playboy* causes marriage, experts say.

   Use Correlation and **56** or **PLAYBOY** and **109** or **MARRIAGE** to fill in the matrix:

	PLAYBOY	MARRIAGE
PLAYBOY		
MARRIAGE		

   What is the correlation between the *Playboy* circulation rate and the marriage rate? _____

   Is it significant? **(circle one)**   YES   NO

   Use the Regression function to fill in this diagram:

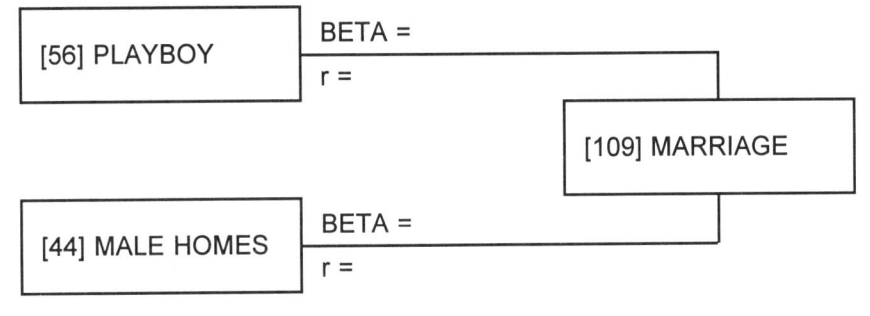

   R-SQ =

   [56] PLAYBOY — BETA = , r = → [109] MARRIAGE

   [44] MALE HOMES — BETA = , r = → [109] MARRIAGE

   What is the combined effect of these two independent variables? _____

   What is the independent or net effect of Playboy? _____

Part VI - *MULTI-VARIATE ANALYSIS*   189.

Worksheets - Exercise 17

Significant? (circle one)   YES   NO

What is the independent or net effect of male homes? _____

Significant? (circle one)   YES   NO

Would you challenge the news report in light of this regression analysis? Explain.

3. **Tales of the Old West:** The lack of churches was the real reason the Old West was so violent.

   Fill in this regression diagram:

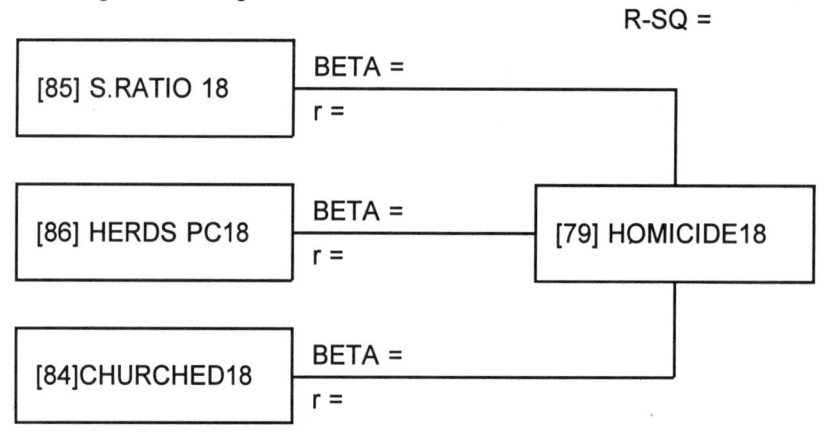

   R-SQ =

   [85] S.RATIO 18 — BETA = , r = — [79] HOMICIDE18

   [86] HERDS PC18 — BETA = , r = — [79] HOMICIDE18

   [84] CHURCHED18 — BETA = , r =

   What is the combined effect of these three independent variables? _____

   What is the independent or net effect of **S.RATIO 18**? _____

   Significant? (circle one)   YES   NO

   What is the independent or net effect of **HERDS PC18**? _____

   Significant? (circle one)   YES   NO

Name: _____   ***Worksheets*** - Exercise 17

What is the independent or net effect of **CHURCHED18**? _____

Significant? (circle one)   YES   NO

Would you challenge the historical claims about churches in light of this regression analysis? Explain.

4. **Tales of the Old West:** Alcohol played a major role in making the Old West so violent.

Fill in this regression diagram:

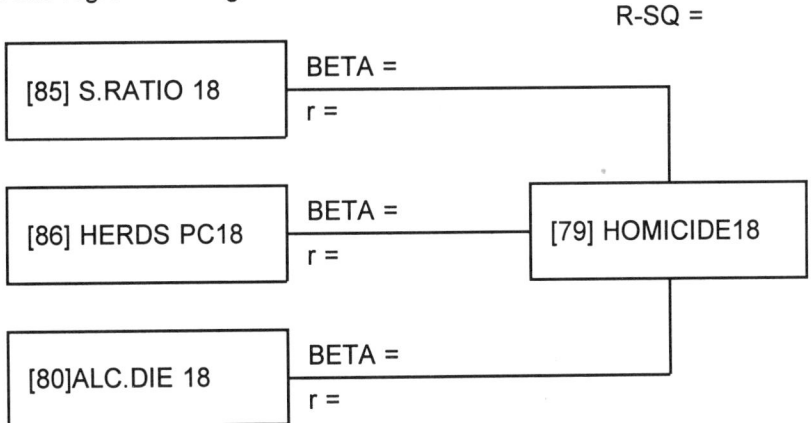

R-SQ = _____

```
[85] S.RATIO 18   ──BETA =──┐
                     r =    │
                            │
[86] HERDS PC18  ──BETA =──┼── [79] HOMICIDE18
                     r =    │
                            │
[80] ALC.DIE 18  ──BETA =──┘
                     r =
```

What is the combined effect of these three independent variables? _____

What is the independent or net effect of **S.RATIO 18**? _____

Significant? (circle one)   YES   NO

What is the independent or net effect of **HERDS PC18**? _____

Significant? (circle one)   YES   NO

Part VI - *MULTI-VARIATE ANALYSIS*

Worksheets - Exercise 17

What is the independent or net effect of **ALC.DIE 18**? _____

Significant? (circle one)   YES   NO

Would you challenge the historical claims about alcohol in light of this regression analysis? Explain.

APPENDIX A: *INDEPENDENT PROJECTS*

There are many variables in each of the three data sets that have been little used, or not used at all, in exercises. Many of these could provide the basis for an independent research project. Such a project need not be limited to your present course or to other courses in criminology. You could use your findings to write papers for other social science courses or for writing courses.

The following suggestions might help you identify some suitable projects.

◆ GUN CONTROL ◆

In the **NORC** data file, **14** or **GUN LAW?**: *Would you favor or oppose a law which would require a person to obtain a police permit before he or she could buy a gun?*

FAVOR	81.6%
OPPOSE	18.4%

Be sure to check gun owners, hunters, and region. You might want to compare regional differences here with regional patterns of hunting in the **FIFTYC** data file.

◆ CAPITAL PUNISHMENT ◆

In the **NORC** data file, **7** or **EXECUTE?**: *Do you favor or oppose the death penalty for persons convicted of murder?*

FAVOR	77.6%
OPPOSE	22.4%

Write a paper reporting who is more favorable to capital punishment. Be sure to check sex, race and church attendance. You also will want to compare these findings with those for college students.

In the **COLLEGEC** data file, **8** or **EXECUTE?**: *Do you favor or oppose the death penalty for persons convicted of murder?*

FAVOR	74.8%
OPPOSE	25.2%

APPENDIX B: CODEBOOKS

SHORT LABEL: NORC

1) FEAR WALK
2) BURGLED?
3) ROBBED?
4) KNOW MURD.
5) COPS HIT?
6) COURTS?
7) EXECUTE?
8) CRIME $
9) DRUGS $
10) GRASS?
11) GO TO BARS
12) DRINK?
13) DRUNK
14) GUN LAW?
15) OWN GUN?
16) HUNT?
17) VETERAN?
18) REGION
19) PLACE SIZE
20) SEX PARTNR
21) SEX
22) RACE
23) WH/AF-A
24) WIRE TAP?
25) AGE
26) FAMILY $
27) INCOME 16
28) EDUCATION
29) MOM FAMILY
30) WHY NO DAD
31) # CHILDREN
32) RELIGION
33) CH ATTEND
34) HAPPY?
35) MARITAL
36) SINGLE/MAR

SHORT LABEL: FIFTYC

1) Case ID
2) #LARCENY
3) POP 1990
4) POP GO 90
5) C.RATE
6) V.CRIME
7) P.CRIME
8) HOMICIDE
9) RAPE
10) ROBBERY
11) ASSAULT
12) BURGLARY
13) LARCENY
14) AUTO THEFT
15) HOMICIDE82
16) HOMICIDE60
17) HOMICIDE40
18) % WHITE
19) %AFRICAN-A
20) % ASIAN
21) %NATIVE AM
22) % HISPANIC
23) COPS/10000
24) JAILERS
25) % RURAL
26) % METROPOL
27) AGE 5-17
28) DENSITY
29) CROWDED
30) $PER CAPIT
31) HOME VALUE
32) RENT
33) HOMELESS
34) WELFARE $
35) % AFDC
36) FOOD STAMP
37) % UNEMPLOY
38) $ WORKERS
39) % POOR
40) DIVORCE
41) % DIVORCED
42) COUPLES
43) % FEMHEAD
44) MALE HOMES
45) % SINGLE
46) %SINGLEMEN
47) %SINGL FEM
48) % COLLEGE
49) % DROPOUTS
50) ABORTION
51) % NO RELIG
52) % JEWISH
53) % CATHOLIC
54) % BAPTIST
55) CH.MEMBER
56) PLAYBOY
57) TV DISHES
58) FLD&STREAM
59) COSMO
60) PICKUPS
61) HUNTING
62) FISHING
63) VETERANS
64) PEACE CORP
65) COKE USERS
66) DRUG EDUC.
67) LIQUOR
68) BEER
69) WINE
70) % WINE
71) % BEER
72) NEW HOMES
73) WARM WINTR
74) ELEVATION
75) AIDS DEATH
76) SOUTHNESS
77) SO.ACCENTS
78) GUN KILL18
79) HOMICIDE18
80) ALC.DIE 18
81) POP GO1860

82) OLD WEST18
83) NEWNESS 18
84) CHURCHED18
85) S.RATIO 18
86) HERDS PC18
87) %BLACK1860
88) %LOCALS 20
89) BURGLARY23
90) LARCENY23
91) POP GO 20

92) BURGLARY40
93) LARCENY 40
94) POP GO 40
95) NOT MOVE40
96) BURGLARY60
97) LARCENY 60
98) NO MOVE 60
99) POP GO 60
100) POP GO 80
101) LARCENY 82

102) BURGLARY82
103) BURGLARY86
104) BURGLARY90
105) CIRRHOSIS
106) % FEM.WORK
107) BURGLARY88
108) BUR.CHANGE
109) MARRIAGE
110) SYPHILIS

SHORT LABEL: **COLLEGEC**

1) TICKET?
2) PICKED UP?
3) SHOPLIFT?
4) DRINK?
5) THROW UP?
6) POT NOW
7) COKE NOW

8) EXECUTE?
9) WHERE LIVE
10) SEX
11) WH/ASIAN
12) FAMILY $
13) MOM ONLY
14) STUDY TIME

15) GRADE PT
16) EMPLOYED?
17) OWN CAR?
18) SEX PARTNR
19) SMOKE?

SHORT LABEL: **HISCHOOL**

1) LAW TROUBL
2) CUT CLASS?
3) DRINK/30
4) MARIJUANA
5) SEX
6) RACE/ETH
7) -REGION

8) MOM'S ED.
9) DAD'S ED.
10) FAMILY SES
11) GRADES
12) HOMEWORK
13) CH.ATTEND
14) CRUISING

15) HANGIN'OUT
16) TO COLLEGE
17) ON PHONE
18) SPORTS?
19) LUCK/WORK

Appendix B - *CODEBOOKS*

LONG LABEL: NORC

1) FEAR WALK
Is there any area right around here — that is, within a mile — where you would be afraid to walk alone at night?

2) BURGLED?
During the last year — that is, between March and now — did anyone break into or somehow illegally get into your (apartment/home)?

3) ROBBED?
During the last year, did anyone take something directly from you by using force — such as a stickup, mugging, or threat?

4) KNOW MURD.
Within the past 12 months, how many people have you known personally that were victims of homicide?

5) COPS HIT?
Are there any situations you can imagine in which you would approve of a policeman striking an adult male citizen?

6) COURTS?
In general, do you think the courts in this area deal too harshly or not harshly enough with criminals?

7) EXECUTE?
Do you favor or oppose the death penalty for persons convicted of murder?

8) CRIME $
Spending on halting the rising crime rate

9) DRUGS $
Spending on dealing with drug addiction

10) GRASS?
Do you think the use of marijuana should be made legal or not?

11) GO TO BARS
HOW OFTEN: Go to a bar or tavern?

12) DRINK?
Do you ever have occasion to use any alcoholic beverages such as liquor, wine, or beer, or are you a total abstainer?

13) DRUNK
Of those who drink: "Do you sometimes drink more than you think you should?"

14) GUN LAW?
Would you favor or oppose a law which would require a person to obtain a police permit before he or she could buy a gun?

15) OWN GUN?
Do you happen to have in your home (IF HOUSE: or garage) any guns or revolvers?

16) HUNT?
Do you (or does your husband/wife) go hunting?

17) VETERAN?
Have you ever been on active duty for military training or service for two consecutive months or more?

18) REGION
REGION OF INTERVIEW

19) PLACE SIZE
SIZE OF COMMUNITY

20) SEX PARTNR
How many sex partners have you had in the last 12 months?

21) SEX
RESPONDENT'S SEX

22) RACE
RESPONDENT'S RACE

23) WH/AF-A
RESPONDENT'S RACE

24) WIRE TAP?
Everything considered, would you say that, in general, you approve or disapprove of wiretapping?

25) AGE
RESPONDENT'S AGE

26) FAMILY $
In which of these groups did your total family income, from all sources, fall last year, before taxes that is?

27) INCOME 16
Thinking about the time when you were 16 years old, compared with American families in general then, would you say your family income was — far below average, below average, average, above average, or far above average?

28) EDUCATION
RESPONDENT'S EDUCATION

29) MOM FAMILY
Were you living with both your own mother and father around the time you were 16? (IF NO: With whom were you living around that time?)

30) WHY NO DAD
IF NOT LIVING WITH BOTH OWN MOTHER AND FATHER: What happened?

31) # CHILDREN
How many children have you ever had? Please count all that were born alive at any time (including any you had from a previous marriage).

32) RELIGION
What is your religious preference? Is it Protestant, Catholic, Jewish, some other religion, or no religion?

33) CH ATTEND
How often do you attend religious services?

34) HAPPY?
Taken all together, how would you say things are these days — would you say that you are very happy, pretty happy, or not too happy?

35) MARITAL
Are you currently — married, widowed, divorced, separated, or have you never been married?

36) SINGLE/MAR
NEVER MARRIED=SINGLE/CURRENTLY MARRIED=MARRIED

LONG LABEL: **FIFTYC**

1) Case ID

2) #LARCENY
1990: NUMBER OF LARCENY-THEFTS REPORTED TO THE POLICE (UCR, 1991)

3) POP 1990
1990: POPULATION IN THOUSANDS (CENSUS)

4) POP GO 90
1980-90: PERCENT GROWTH (OR DECLINE) IN POPULATION (CENSUS)

5) C.RATE
1992: CRIMES PER 100,000 (UCR,93)

6) V.CRIME
1992: VIOLENT CRIMES PER 100,000 (UCR,93)

7) P.CRIME
1992: PROPERTY CRIMES PER 100,000 (UCR,93)

8) HOMICIDE
1992: HOMICIDES PER 100,000 (UCR,93)

9) RAPE
1992: RAPES PER 100,000 (UCR,93)

10) ROBBERY
1992: ROBBERIES PER 100,000 (UCR,93)

11) ASSAULT
1992: ASSAULTS PER 100,000 (UCR,93)

12) BURGLARY
1992: BURGLARIES PER 100,000 (UCR,93)

13) LARCENY
1992: LARCENIES PER 100,000 (UCR,93)

14) AUTO THEFT
1992: VEHICLE THEFTS PER 100,000 (UCR,93)

15) HOMICIDE82
1982: HOMICIDES PER 100,000 POPULATION (UCR,83)

16) HOMICIDE60
1960: HOMICIDES PER 100,000

17) HOMICIDE40
1940: HOMICIDES PER 100,000 POPULATION

18) % WHITE
1990: PERCENT WHITE (CENSUS)

19) %AFRICAN-A
1990: PERCENT AFRICAN-AMERICAN (CENSUS)

20) % ASIAN
1990: PERCENT ASIAN (CENSUS)

21) %NATIVE AM
1990: PERCENT NATIVE AMERICAN (CENSUS)

22) % HISPANIC
1990: PERCENT HISPANIC — HISPANICS MAY BE OF ANY RACE (CENSUS)

23) COPS/10000
1990: STATE AND LOCAL LAW ENFORCEMENT OFFICERS PER 10,000 (S.P.R. 1991)

24) JAILERS
1988: JAIL AND PRISON OFFICERS PER 10,000 POPULATION (S.A.,1991)

25) % RURAL
1990: PERCENT OF POPULATION LIVING IN RURAL AREAS — UNINCORPORATED OR POPULATION LESS THAN 2500 (CENSUS)

26) % METROPOL
1988: PERCENT OF THE POPULATION LIVING IN METROPOLITAN STATISTICAL AREAS (S.A.,1990)

27) AGE 5-17
1990: PERCENT OF POPULATION AGE 5-17 (CENSUS)

28) DENSITY
1990: POPULATION PER SQUARE MILE (CENSUS)

29) CROWDED
1990: PERCENT OF OCCUPIED HOUSING UNITS WITH MORE THAN 1 PERSON PER ROOM (CENSUS)

30) $PER CAPIT
1987: PER CAPITA INCOME (S.A., 1991)

31) HOME VALUE
1990: MEDIAN VALUE OF OWNER-OCCUPIED HOUSING UNITS (CENSUS)

32) RENT
1990: MEDIAN MONTHLY RENT FOR RENTER-OCCUPIED HOUSING UNITS (CENSUS)

33) HOMELESS
1990: NUMBER OF HOMELESS PER 10,000 POPULATION (S.P.R.)

34) WELFARE $
1989: PER CAPITA STATE SPENDING ON WELFARE (CENSUS REPORT, "GOVERNMENT FINANCES," 1990)

35) % AFDC
1988: PERCENT OF ALL HOUSHOLDS RECEIVING AID TO FAMILIES WITH DEPENDENT CHILDREN (AFDC) (S.P.R., 1991)

36) FOOD STAMP
1990: PERCENT OF POPULATION RECEIVING FOOD STAMPS (S.P.R., 1991)

37) % UNEMPLOY
1991: PERCENT OF CIVILIAN LABOR FORCE UNEMPLOYED (E&E,11/91)

38) $ WORKERS
1991: AVERAGE WEEKLY EARNINGS OF PRODUCTION WORKERS ON MANUFACTURING PAYROLLS (E&E 11/91)

39) % POOR
1990: PERCENT OF POPULATION BELOW OFFICIAL POVERTY LINE (CENSUS)

40) DIVORCE
1989: DIVORCES PER 1,000 POPULATION (S.A., 1991)

41) % DIVORCED
1990: PERCENT OF THOSE 15 AND OVER WHO CURRENTLY ARE DIVORCED (CENSUS)

42) COUPLES
1990: PERCENT OF HOUSEHOLDS OCCUPIED BY A MARRIED COUPLE (CENSUS)

43) % FEMHEAD
1990: PERCENT OF HOUSEHOLDS OCCUPIED BY A WOMAN AND HER CHILDREN (CENSUS)

44) MALE HOMES
1990: PERCENT OF HOUSEHOLDS WITHOUT AN ADULT FEMALE RESIDENT (CENSUS)

45) % SINGLE
1990: PERCENT OF PERSONS 15 AND OVER WHO HAVE NEVER BEEN MARRIED (CENSUS)

46) %SINGLEMEN
1990: PERCENT OF MALES 15 AND OVER WHO HAVE NEVER MARRIED (CENSUS)

47) %SINGL FEM
1990: PERCENT OF FEMALES AGE 15 AND OVER WHO HAVE NEVER MARRIED (CENSUS)

48) % COLLEGE
1990: PERCENT OF POPULATION 25 AND OLDER WHO HAVE A COLLEGE DEGREE (CENSUS)

49) % DROPOUTS
1990: PERCENT OF PERSONS WHO LEFT SCHOOL WITHOUT GRADUATING FROM HIGH SCHOOL (SA, 1993)

50) ABORTION
1988: ABORTIONS PER 1,000 LIVE BIRTHS (S.A., 1991)

51) % NO RELIG
1990: PERCENT OF THE POPULATION WHO SAY THEY HAVE NO RELIGION (KOSMIN)

52) % JEWISH
1990: PERCENT OF THE POPULATION WHO GIVE THEIR RELIGIOUS PREFERENCES AS JEWISH (KOSMIN)

53) % CATHOLIC
1990: PERCENT OF THE POPULATION WHO GIVE THEIR RELIGIOUS PREFERENCE AS CATHOLIC (KOSMIN)

54) % BAPTIST
1990: PERCENT OF THE POPULATION WHO GIVE THEIR RELIGIOUS PREFERENCE AS BAPTIST (KOSMIN)

55) CH.MEMBER
1990: PERCENT OF POPULATION BELONGING TO A LOCAL CHURCH (CHURCH)

56) PLAYBOY
1990: PLAYBOY CIRCULATION PER 100,000 POPULATION (ABC)

57) TV DISHES
1990: SATELLITE TV DISHES PER 10,000 (ORBIT MAG. 3/1991)

58) FLD&STREAM
1990: CIRCULATION OF FIELD & STREAM MAGAZINE PER 100,000 (ABC)

59) COSMO
1990: CIRCULATION OF COSMOPOLITAN MAGAZINE PER 100,000 (ABC)

60) PICKUPS
1989: PICKUPS PER 1,000 POPULATION (HIGHWAY STATISTICS, 1989)

61) HUNTING
1990: NUMBER OF RESIDENTS WHO PURCHASED HUNTING LICENSES PER 1,000 POPULATION (U.S.FISH & WILDLIFE)

62) FISHING
1990: NUMBER OF RESIDENTS WHO PURCHASED FISHING LICENSES PER 1,000 (U.S.FISH & WILDLIFE)

63) VETERANS
1988: VETERANS PER 1,000 POPULATION (S.A.1990)

64) PEACE CORP
1985: TOTAL RESIDENTS WHO JOINED PEACE CORPS 1961-1985 PER 10,000 (THE PEACE CORPS, IN USA TODAY:10/8/85)

65) COKE USERS
1990: COCAINE ADDICTS PER 1,000 POPULATION (SENATE JUDICIARY COMMITTEE, USA TODAY:8/6/90)

66) DRUG EDUC.
1990: SCHOOL FUNDS PER STUDENT SPENT ON DRUG EDUCATION IN DOLLARS (SENATE JUDICIARY COMMITTEE, USA TODAY, 9/6/90)

67) LIQUOR
1989: GALLONS OF ALCOHOLIC BEVERAGES CONSUMED PER PERSON 16 AND OVER (HCSR, 1993)

68) BEER
1989: GALLONS OF BEER CONSUMED PER PERSON 16 AND OVER (HCSR, 1993)

69) WINE
1989: GALLONS OF WINE CONSUMED PER PERSON 16 AND OVER (HCSR, 1993)

70) % WINE
1989: THE PERCENT OF ALCOHOLIC BEVERAGES CONSUMED THAT WAS WINE (HCSR, 1993)

71) % BEER
1989: THE PERCENTAGE OF ALCOHOLIC BEVERAGES CONSUMED THAT WAS BEER (HCSR, 1993)

72) NEW HOMES
1990: PERCENT OF ALL HOUSING UNITS CONSTRUCTED SINCE 1980 (CENSUS)

73) WARM WINTR
AVERAGE JANUARY LOW TEMPERATURE

74) ELEVATION
APPROXIMATE MEAN ELEVATION IN FEET

75) AIDS DEATH
1982-1989: DEATHS FROM AIDS PER 100,000 POPULATION (SMAD, 1991)

76) SOUTHNESS
DEGREES OF LATITUDE SOUTH OF THE NORTH POLE, BASED ON LOCATION OF STATE CAPITAL. NEW MEX. = COLOR.; ARIZ = UTAH. Omitted cases: Alaska, Hawaii.

77) SO.ACCENTS
1990: CIRCULATION OF SOUTHERN ACCENTS MAGAZINE PER 100,000 (ABC)

78) GUN KILL18
1860: DEATHS FROM ACCIDENTAL GUNSHOT WOUNDS PER 100,000 (CENSUS)

79) HOMICIDE18
1860: HOMICIDES PER 100,000 (CENSUS)

80) ALC.DIE 18
1860: NUMBER OF DEATHS FROM "DELIRIUM TREMENS" & "INTEMPERANCE" PER 100,000 (CENSUS)

81) POP GO1860
1850-60: PERCENT POPULATION GROWTH (-DECLINE) (CENSUS)

82) OLD WEST18
DEGREES OF LONGITUDE WEST OF THE PRIME MERIDIAN OF STATE CAPITAL

83) NEWNESS 18
1860: NEWNESS OF STATEHOOD: YEAR OF STATEHOOD MINUS 1787

84) CHURCHED18
1860: RELIGIOUS ADHERENTS PER 1,000 POPULATION (F & S)

85) S.RATIO 18
1860: NUMBER OF MALES PER 100 FEMALES (CENSUS)

86) HERDS PC18
1860: BEEF CATTLE, SHEEP AND PIGS PER CAPITA (CENSUS)

87) %BLACK1860
1860: PERCENT BLACK (CENSUS)

88) %LOCALS 20
1920: PERCENT OF POPULATION BORN IN STATE OF CURRENT RESIDENCE (CENSUS)

89) BURGLARY23
1923: PERSONS SENT UP FOR BURGLARY PER 100,000 (P.CENSUS)

90) LARCENY23
1923:PERSONS SENT UP FOR LARCENY PER 100,000 (P.CENSUS)

91) POP GO 20
PERCENT POPULATION GROWTH (OR -DECLINE), 1910-1920 (CENSUS)

92) BURGLARY40
1940: BURGLARIES PER 100,000 (UCR, 1941)

93) LARCENY 40
1940: LARCENIES PER 100,000 (UCR, 1941)

94) POP GO 40
PERCENTAGE INCREASE (OR -DECREASE) IN POPULATION SIZE, 1930-1940 (CENSUS)

95) NOT MOVE40
1940: PERCENT OF POPULATION WHO HAVE NOT MOVED SINCE 1935 (CENSUS)

96) BURGLARY60
1960: BURGLARIES PER 100,000 (UCR, 1961)

97) LARCENY 60
1960: LARCENY ($50 AND OVER) PER 100,000 (UCR, 1961)

98) NO MOVE 60
1960: PERCENT LIVING IN SAME HOUSE AS IN 1955 (CENSUS)

99) POP GO 60
1960: PERCENTAGE POPULATION INCREASE OR (-) DECREASE 1950-60 (CENSUS)

100) POP GO 80
% POPULATION GROWTH (OR DECLINE) 1970-80 (CENSUS)

101) LARCENY 82
1982: LARCENIES PER 100,000 POPULATION (UCR, 1983)

102) BURGLARY82
1982: BURGLARIES PER 100,000 POPULATION (UCR, 1983)

103) BURGLARY86
1986: BURGLARIES PER 100,000

104) BURGLARY90
1990: BURGLARIES PER 100,000 (UCR, 1991)

105) CIRRHOSIS
1986: DEATHS FROM CIRRHOSIS OF THE LIVER PER 100,000 (S.A.,1990)

106) % FEM.WORK
1989: PERCENT OF ADULT FEMALES IN THE LABOR FORCE (SMAD, 1991)

107) BURGLARY88
1988: BURGLARIES PER 100,000 POPULATION (UCR, 1989)

108) BUR.CHANGE
1982-1990: DECLINE (OR INCREASE) IN THE BURGLARY RATE (UCR, 1983-91)

109) MARRIAGE
1989: MARRIAGES PER 1,000 POPULATION (S.A.,1991)

110) SYPHILIS
1988: REPORTED NUMBER OF CASES OF SYPHILIS PER 100,000 POPULATION (SMAD, 1991)

LONG LABEL: **COLLEGEC**

1) TICKET?
Have you ever received a ticket, or been charged by the police, for a traffic violation — other than illegal parking?

2) PICKED UP?
Were you ever picked up, or charged, by the police for any other reason, whether or not you were guilty?

3) SHOPLIFT?
Have you ever shoplifted?

4) DRINK?
Whether or not you ever have drunk alcoholic beverages such as liquor, wine, or beer, do you do so now or are you a total abstainer?

5) THROW UP?
During the past year have you been nauseated or vomited due to your drinking or drug use?

6) POT NOW
Has smoked marijuana in past year?

7) COKE NOW
Has used cocaine (crack, rock, freebase) in past year

8) EXECUTE?
Do you favor or oppose the death penalty for persons convicted of murder?

9) WHERE LIVE
Do you live at home, in a dorm or where?

10) SEX
Sex:

11) WH/ASIAN
RACE: WHITE OR ASIAN (INSUFFICIENT CASES OF OTHER RACE & ETHNIC GROUPS)

12) FAMILY $
Thinking about your parents, or the people with whom you lived during high school, compared with other American families, would you say their income was below average or above?

13) MOM ONLY
When you were 16, were you living with both your father and your mother? If not, with whom were you living?

14) STUDY TIME
During an average week, how many hours each week do you spend studying for college?

15) GRADE PT
What is your GPA (Grade Point Average)

16) EMPLOYED?
Are you employed?

17) OWN CAR?
At present, do you have your own car?

18) SEX PARTNR
How many different sexual partners have you ever had in your life?

19) SMOKE?
Do you smoke?

LONG LABEL: **HISCHOOL**

1) LAW TROUBL
I have been in serious trouble with the law

2) CUT CLASS?
Every once in a while I cut a class

3) DRINK/30
On how many occasions (if any) have you had alcohol to drink (beer, wine, liquor) during the past thirty days?

4) MARIJUANA
On how many occasions (if any) have you used HASHISH (hash) or MARIJUANA (grass, pot, dope)?

5) SEX
SEX OF RESPONDENT

6) RACE/ETH
RACE/ETHNICITY OF RESPONDENT

7) -REGION
REGION

8) MOM'S ED.
What was the highest level of education your mother (stepmother or female guardian) completed?

9) DAD'S ED.
What was the highest level of education your father (stepfather or male guardian) completed?

10) FAMILY SES
QUARTILE CODING OF COMPOSITE VARIABLE FAMILY SOCIO-ECONOMIC STATUS

11) GRADES
HIGH GRADES: MOSTLY B'S AND BETTER/B'S/C'S AND WORSE

12) HOMEWORK
During an average week, about how many hours do you spend doing homework?

13) CH.ATTEND
In the past year, about how often have you attended religious services?

14) CRUISING
How often do you just drive or ride around (alone or with friends)

15) HANGIN'OUT
How often do you spend time visiting with friends at a local gathering place

16) TO COLLEGE
Do you plan to go to college at some time in the future?

17) ON PHONE
How often do you talk with friends on the telephone

18) SPORTS?
Have you participated in ... Varsity athletic teams?

19) LUCK/WORK
Good luck is more important than hard work for success

SOURCES

The source of each variable in the **FIFTYC** data file is indicated in its long label. Often these are abbreviated. A complete key to these abbreviations follows.

ABC: Audit Bureau of Circulations Blue Book, 1990.

CENSUS: The summary volumes of the U.S. Census for the indicated year.

CHRON.: The Chronicle of Higher Education Almanac for the indicated year.

CHURCH: Bradley, Martin B., Dale E. Jones, Mac Lynn and Lou McNeil, Churches and Church Membership in the United States, 1990. Atlanta, Glen Mary Research Center, 1992..

E & E: U.S. Bureau of Labor Statistics. *Employment and Earnings*, issued monthly.

F & S: Roger Finke and Rodney Stark, The Churching of America - 1776-1990: Winners and Losers in Our Religious Economy. Rutgers University Press, 1992.

HCSR: Healthcare State Rankings, 1993. Morgan Quitno.

KOSMIN: Kosmin, Barry A. 1991. Research Report: The National Survey of Religious Identification, New York: CUNY Graduate Center.

S.A.: Statistical Abstract of the United States for the indicated year.

SMAD: State and Metropolitan Area Data Book, 1991.

S.P.R.: State Policy Reference for the indicated year.

UCR: The Uniform Crime Report published in the year indicated.

LICENSE AGREEMENT

READ THIS LICENSE AGREEMENT CAREFULLY BEFORE OPENING THE DISKETTE PACKAGE. BY OPENING THIS PACKAGE YOU ACCEPT THE TERMS OF THIS AGREEMENT.

MicroCase® Corporation, hereinafter called the Licensor, grants the purchaser of this software, hereinafter called the Licensee, the right to use and reproduce the software entitled **Criminology: *An Introduction Through MicroCase*,** in accordance with the following terms and conditions:

Permitted Uses

- You may use this software only for educational purposes.

- You may use the software on any compatible computer, provided the software is used on only one computer and by one user at a time.

- You may make a backup copy of the diskette(s).

Prohibited Uses

- You may not use this software for any purposes other than educational purposes.

- You may not make copies of the documentation or program disk, except backup copies as described above.

- You may not distribute, rent, sub-license or lease the software or documentation.

- You may not alter, modify, or adapt the software or documentation, including, but not limited to, translating, decompiling, disassembling, or creating derivative works.

- You may not use the software on a network, file server, or virtual disk.

THIS AGREEMENT IS EFFECTIVE UNTIL TERMINATED. IT WILL TERMINATE IF LICENSEE FAILS TO COMPLY WITH ANY TERM OR CONDITION OF THIS AGREEMENT. LICENSEE MAY TERMINATE IT AT ANY OTHER TIME BY DESTROYING THE SOFTWARE TOGETHER WITH ALL COPIES. IF THIS AGREEMENT IS TERMINATED BY LICENSOR, LICENSEE AGREES TO EITHER DESTROY OR RETURN THE ORIGINAL AND ALL EXISTING COPIES OF THE SOFTWARE TO THE LICENSOR WITHIN FIVE (5) DAYS AFTER RECEIVING NOTICE OF TERMINATION FROM THE LICENSOR.

MicroCase Corporation retains all rights not expressly granted in this License Agreement. Nothing in the License Agreement constitutes a waiver of MicroCase Corporation's rights under the U.S. copyright laws or any other federal or state Law.

Should you have any questions concerning this Agreement, you may contact MicroCase Corporation by calling (800) 682-7367.